Airportness

Airportness

The Nature of Flight

Christopher Schaberg

Octavia Butts
Nola

Bloomsbury Academic
An imprint of Bloomsbury Publishing Inc

B L O O M S B U R Y
NEW YORK · LONDON · OXFORD · NEW DELHI · SYDNEY

Bloomsbury Academic

An imprint of Bloomsbury Publishing Inc

1385 Broadway	50 Bedford Square
New York	London
NY 10018	WC1B 3DP
USA	UK

www.bloomsbury.com

BLOOMSBURY and the Diana logo are trademarks of Bloomsbury Publishing Plc

First published 2017

Library of Congress Cataloging-in-Publication Data

Names: Schaberg, Christopher, author.
Title: Airportness: the nature of flight / Christopher Schaberg.
Description: New York: Bloomsbury Academic, 2017. | Includes bibliographical references and index.
Identifiers: LCCN 2017005080| ISBN 9781501325700 (hardback) | ISBN 9781501325694 (paperback) | ISBN 9781501325724 (epdf)
Subjects: LCSH: Airports–Social aspects. | Air travel–Social aspects. | BISAC: LITERARY CRITICISM / Semiotics & Theory. | NATURE / Ecology.
Classification: LCC HE9797 .S329 2017 | DDC 387.7/36–dc23 LC record available at https://lccn.loc.gov/2017005080

ISBN: HB: 978-1-5013-2570-0
PB: 978-1-5013-2569-4
ePub: 978-1-5013-2571-7
ePDF: 978-1-5013-2572-4

Cover design: Eleanor Rose
Cover image © Jorge Díaz/Creative Commons

Typeset by Deanta Global Publishing Services, Chennai, India
Printed and bound in the United States of America

To find out more about our authors and books visit www.bloomsbury.com. Here you will find extracts, author interviews, details of forthcoming events, and the option to sign up for our newsletters.

For Camille

Contents

Preflight 1

Ride to the Airport 4

Curbside 12

Boarding Pass 16

Security 21

Walk to the Gate 25

People Watching 29

Attack 30

Waiting 33

Workers 35

Art 36

Gate Change 38

Gate Lice 39

Fishing Shirts 40

Runway 43

Holding 47

Takeoff 49

Window Seat 50

Sunrise 53

Armrests 55

New Planes 59

Airplane Reading I 61

Consider the Lavatory 70

Snacking 74

Initial Descent 75

Connection 78

Play 82

Sparrows 84

Twitter 87

Breakfast 88

747 89

Colin Farrell 91

In-flight Entertainment I: *Somewhere* 93

In-flight Entertainment II: *The Force Awakens* 97

Airplane Reading II 101

Plane Sighting 108

Higher Still 115

Entanglements 118

In-flight Entertainment III: *United 93* 131

Old Planes 139

Gender 141

Water Landing 143

Arrival 148

Destination 149

Baggage 154

Exit 158

Home 160

Acknowledgments 169

Bibliography 170

Index 177

Each time I get on a plane

I miss everybody.

—EILEEN MYLES

Preflight

It's dark out, and quiet except for the gurgling of a small refrigerator in the corner of the room. I'm in bed and my alarm won't go off for another hour, but my mind is buzzing in anticipation of the trip to come. This is not my bed, and the pillow is unfamiliar—I'm in a hotel. However, it's not these things that have woken me up. It's the airport calling me: bright screens, the distant rumble of jet engines, and impersonal walkways.

Do you remember your first time in an airport? Do you recall the airport itself, or just the time in flight? Was it during the so-called golden age of air travel, post-9/11, or somewhere in the messy in-between? Do you ever imagine the future of flight, beyond anything we've experienced so far? What does it look like?

These questions play in my mind as I lie here listening to occasional, muffled highway sounds. It's 3:21 in the morning, and I'm wide awake when I should be asleep. I have to be in a cab and on the way to the airport in just under an hour. My alarm is set for 4:05, but it's pointless to have the chime go off if I won't even be asleep when the minute strikes. Still, there's a chance that I will doze, perhaps even fall into a deep sleep before being jerked out of my reverie and back into airport time, where a plane is being prepared for me. Flying is funny like this: it infiltrates you long before you ever set foot in the airport, or in an airplane.

Each day, countless times over, the miracle of human air travel is reduced to the existential drag of the early morning flight, dependent on the predawn slog—so many private rituals and compromises involving sleep (or the lack thereof), tiptoeing around still slumbering family members, roommates, or garish hotel furniture; the quick shower or decision not to (which will be regretted later, on the plane).

Airports concentrate and make plain so much of modern life: the food we eat there, how we entertain and distract ourselves, the ways attitudes and judgments are expressed . . . airports are a snapshot of contemporary culture at work. Airports are also critical spaces where we might learn how to coexist on this planet—with other people, as well as with other species and alongside myriad other migration routes. What happens at airports does not stay at airports—as much as we may wish that were the case, sometimes. Airports spread out into our lives. They have become landscape features as well as symbols of various things, from prosperity and excess to boredom and waste. We've internalized airports—we know them by their scents and sounds. Airports come to be test sites where many of our best and worst behaviors play out. They are highly organized spaces that can be full of civil interactions, clear communication, and generosity; they can also become tangled in logistical knots and overflow with spite, pettiness, impatience, and acrimony.

The forty-fifth president of the United States, Donald Trump, has claimed that American airports are obsolete and in desperate need of overhauling. Air travel can be maddening and can induce claustrophobia—but is it really fair to label functioning airports as outdated? Or are they just imperfect sites riddled with contingencies that, against all odds, tend to work pretty well most of the time? Aren't airports almost perfect indicators of who we *are* in the early twenty-first century? Trump also seems to have an idea of what truly "incredible" airports would be like, and how the United States should try to achieve such things. But this vision may end up more like science fiction—or a classist dystopia—than actual progress. Either way, airports register our behaviors and predilections. Airports measure our lives, in different directions and divergent ways.

At the airport "preflight" means one thing: sheets of information handed to the crew, boarding calls and congested queues, and catering trucks loading fresh snacks on the plane. But the real effects of preflight can be traced much earlier—going back into your home or hotel room, conditioning your sleep or infecting your insomnia. Preflight can also run out into a widespread sense of urgency and alertness concerning flights overhead or overheard. To be a modern human means to be always somewhat *preflight*: waiting and ready for an airport trip to come, whether this takes shape as a mythically conceived vacation, a potential business trip on the horizon, a rote airport run to pick up a relative, or an unplanned exodus.

This is all part of *airportness*, or how the feel of air travel precedes and extends past the more obvious dimensions and boundaries of flight. Airportness is what is keeping me from sleeping an hour before I need to wake up. It's the faint noise in my head, the lumps in my pillow, and the push and pull of the airplane to come. It is all the flight logistics that go into political campaigns, all the flashy livery and tarmac speeches. It's the regular flight path of an airplane that wakes you up at five in the morning, even when you're not the one flying. This is the nature of flight in the twenty-first century.

Ride to the Airport

"Rides to airports make me quiet and glum" (96). So wrote Don DeLillo in his 1984 novel *White Noise*, a story peppered with trips to the airport and their consequent emotional surges and drains. The airport figures into this novel as a minor character of sorts: a grim, nagging presence on the outskirts of town.

Imagine you are on the way to the airport, alone. What does this feel like to you? What time of day is it? Is it dark out? How did you sleep the night before? Soundly, or were you restless and obsessing about the trip to come? Is it so routine that you can't even conjure any feeling at all, no sense impressions to speak of?

For me, it's usually hard to sleep the night before, and even though I set my alarm, I inevitably wake up long before it sounds. But once I'm up I'm fully alert. I get dressed, and slip outside into the predawn purple. I notice the temperature more than usual—the air is sharp, or thick, or crisp. The pavement is extra hard; condensation sticks more than usual. This is all in anticipation of the airport journey.

A van or sedan pulls up, engine humming and the driver consulting a notepad or tapping at a smartphone. Perhaps there is a GPS aglow on the dashboard. There may be an indefinite airplane logo somewhere on the vehicle, or else no markings at all—purely anonymous conveyance. In either case I get in, and the ride to the airport commences. Light chitchat may follow, or awkward silence.

I'm interested in these sorts of minor details, in what makes an airport what it is, and what constitutes a normal day of air travel—even when, or especially when, these are things we don't think about or don't *want* to think about. You can't fully appreciate airports without considering the ways to and from these spaces, and all the people involved in these transit lines that precede and escape the terminal. And if this sounds unwieldy, good—it is.

On my way to the airport now, I'm thinking of these things, and letting my mind run freely. Part of my goal with this book is that you, too, will let your mind run free when it comes to airports. It's all too easy to make snap judgments and hold instant grudges toward airports and their various aspects. But, slow down and reflect—there's a lot going on here worth lingering on.

First of all, what is an airport?

An airport is undeniably its terminal and concourses. But it does not end there. The airport spreads out of the jet bridges, over the runways, up the control tower, and out into the clouds. It ends up on living room floors, in the form of toy airplanes and play luggage carts. It wends its way onto our smartphones, via airline apps and route maps. It slides through your mail slot in the background of a credit card application: the anonymous flurry of airport activities connotes *mobility, success, freedom*. It pops into view in the subject line of an email from a travel website, in the minimal form of ✈. This is a seemingly simple symbol that whispers, *fly*. And when you are strolling across a street and a glint in the sky catches your eye, the airport is suddenly you, monitoring a flight from the ground (if only subconsciously) for an instant.

The term "airportness" has been used to describe the architectural feel of terminal buildings. Think of vaulted ceilings, plate glass windows with runway views, rows of familiar (if less than comfortable) fixed seats, claustrophobic concourses with cascading gate numbers . . . These are all fairly straightforward signs of airportness. On this ride to the airport, let me tell you more about how I have come to think about this word, airportness.

In this book I adopt and apply the term *airportness* expansively, to mean how it is a general feeling: dispersed, subtle, and arriving in many unexpected forms. Airportness is about how air travel gets in our heads and bodies, how it becomes something *natural*. It's the draw of the airport in the dark, many miles yet down the highway or train track, when you're still on the way. It's on the road signs that are named after airfields or flight, long before these things become visible. But airportness also extends beyond the journey proper.

It happens anytime you hear a plane overhead.

It happens when you see an airport in the background of a commercial or ad.

It happens when you notice (even if you barely register it) a breaking news item about delayed flights or a smoking crash site.

It happens when we joke about cramped airplane seats, or when we complain about awkward seatmate situations long after the flight is over.

It happens in the most passing scene in a movie or television show, when characters arrive or depart in a flash—a whole journey summed up in a one-second shot of teeming airport life.

It happens when our credit cards display airline logos, subtly reminding us of flight every time we buy groceries or gas. Abstract "miles" add up, faint promises of trips to come (or not).

Airportness is how we embody flight even when we're not thinking about it. How we accept it even when we loathe it. How we consume flight—passively, actively, and every way in between—as a part of modern life. Airportness is also about how we treat people: not just in the confined spaces of travel, but in every transitional point in life—which is to say, everywhere and always.

This is the third book I've written about airports. My first book on this subject, called *The Textual Life of Airports*, was an adaptation of a doctoral dissertation I wrote that looked at how airports are represented in American literature. At an earlier point in my life I worked at an airport—stories you can read about in my second book, *The End of Airports*—so I have affinities for and sympathies with everyday life on the tarmac and in the terminal, from a labor standpoint.

At Loyola University New Orleans I teach a class about airports, and these experiences have further shaped how I see air travel as a kind of language that people become fluent in, on their way to their careers or otherwise adult lives. Teaching my students how to "read the culture of flight," I have also thought a lot about how our new digital technologies are bumping up against and shaping how we experience airports. On the first day of class I ask my students to share their own air travel experiences, and how they feel about airports in general. Their responses range from loving flight to hating it, from the pleasures of people watching to the grind of airport waiting. Usually one student has a parent or other relative who is an airline employee. At some point a student will say, with intuitively correct sounding certainty, that human flight is so "unnatural." Why do we think we should be flying, when everything about our creaturely being suggests otherwise? Put simply: we cannot get off the ground using our own appendages, much less survive at 36,000 feet on our own—so why do we even think we should be up there in the first place? *Humans were not made to fly!*

And yet, humans have arrived at the place where we are by way of flight. Our airplanes have become strange prostheses, extensions of our very bodies and ways of being. Aircraft transport us, change us, and provide new points of view. We can see an awareness of this as early as 1941 in a story by F. Scott Fitzgerald, "Three Hours between Planes," which closes with this image: "The plane roared up into the dark sky and its passengers became a different entity from the corporate world below." We see it again, half a century later, in a 1997 poem by Brenda Hillman called "Symmetry Breaking," when an aircraft window opens up a weirdly double aerial sight: "Lots of same Utah over the—not sure what to call it—chicken with the flap of itself on top." The views from above—of stark geography, and of gross airplane food—have become naturalized, mere aspects of modern human life. Likewise, the tilted *T* on the tail of Donald Trump's Boeing 757 is an extension of the person inside, just as the plane itself extends this person to unimaginable heights and destinations. We equate flight with human progress; flight is—or has become, anyway—*natural* to us.

But to say flight is natural isn't to simply accept it, or to merely shrug about a dismal (or desirable, depending on your perspective) state of affairs. It's just to note that this is what we as a species have *done*; this is a way we have decided to migrate on a regular basis—collectively and individually, always entangled. We may decide to change our travel plans; humans might yet recommit to the ground. Or we may find more graceful ways to move through the air. For now, though, flight as we know it is (in) our nature. It's time to contemplate what this means, and how it manifests itself: human flight as *natural*.

During his 2016 presidential bid, Donald Trump often remarked that he wanted to make American airports better. How could this actually take shape, so that people would enjoy working at or passing through airports? This is not a glib query. Can we imagine such a thing? What would it mean to accept flight as a marker of our species, and as something that cannot help but affect and be affected by all other systems of life on this planet? To not only accept this, but perhaps to change things for the better? I pose these questions in all sincerity and earnestness. I am finishing this book as Trump prepares to take office, and while the question of future airports is relatively low on the list of burning questions about how Trump will actually lead, I want to take the time to linger on some of the thornier and more pedestrian aspects of air travel, to examine what takes place within the nature of flight.

This book is for readers who are interested in air travel as a puzzle, a routine, or an everyday miracle. And it is for readers who are curious about the more eccentric edges of ecological thinking: this is nature writing that takes the airport as its wilderness. While in my previous two books I touched on the ecological dimensions of airports and aerial views, in the present book I attempt to bring these considerations into the foreground, ruminating on how in each site and situation this interplay takes place, between airports and something like *nature*. I'm interested in how flight becomes naturalized, how it comes to seem normal and inevitable to us as a species, and what the stakes of this might be. What follows are stories and scenes where air travel meshes or clashes with environmental awareness, where airplane contrails bleed into the horizon like so many more cloud stripes. This is a book about the nature of flight, and I am its nature writer.

Nature writing and eco-criticism are established genres and forms of expression and investigation—especially *American* traditions, from Henry David Thoreau to Terry Tempest Williams and beyond. In this book I think about the airplane journey as another subject of ecological inquiry, following a trail blazed in part by Barry Lopez's stirring essay from 1999, "Flight," in which the writer accompanies cargo shipments around the world on widebody jets, tracing the eerie paths of animals and things around the globe.

If we accept the perhaps odd proposition that technological flight is natural—or at least has become naturalized, as an accepted and vibrant part of our environment—how might we see the effects of this naturalization and entanglement play out in everyday life, art, and culture? How have air travel and all the possible experiences therein become accepted as inevitable, as if biologically determined, and yet often felt as existentially looming, too? How has flight become an indicator of various environmental sensibilities, assumptions, and behaviors—especially in the ramping up of the digital age, when we seem more oblivious to what's outside our screens than ever? We know the twentieth-century story of flight. But what is the appropriate way to understand—and potentially change—air travel in the twenty-first century? *Airportness* takes off from such questions.

This book is limited, partial, and critical; it's also uncertain, meditative, and full of wonder. I know what it's like to be at airports—stuck there or spirited away, by turns—as a worker, as a passenger, or picking up a loved one. But what is this mundane and modern air journey really about? In this book I trace my own ambivalent feelings and thinking around airports, from origin to destination. Take a trip with me, from departure to arrival. Rethink the whole operation to then appreciate it more fully, if also to come away with open questions concerning the nature of flight.

One final note here, as we race along this dimly lit highway: I switch pronouns regularly throughout this book, from *I* to *you* to *we* and back again. This is because while airportness is something that I feel, I trust that you feel it too, in your own ways. And we feel it together, often unconsciously or abstractly. And this "we" is distributed across the millions of travelers and airport and airline workers each day. Air travel privileges the individual, while always ready to switch to the next individual, or to revert to all of us in an instant. So in this book I let the nature of flight infuse me, you, and us by turns.

Are you ready to fly? Here come the exit signs that lead the way to the airport.

Curbside

At the curbside I feel a blend of excitement and sadness—I'm leaving one thing and entering another, and it is never easy to know what to make of this rent in the seam of everyday life. It can be swift or tense, sad or joyful. Of course, for some, this rent *is* everyday life—especially for the many people who work at the airport.

What does the curbside conjure in *your* mind?

When I used to work at the airport, I would observe this charged space from behind my check-in counter. At the curbside, sentiments swirl. Fear, excitement, dread, annoyance, anticipation—these feelings run the gamut of human emotion, and the airport funnels and sorts them, and makes them plain. The curbside is where so many of these feelings take place and are on display, if just for a split second.

The photographer Garry Winogrand noticed this and documented countless banal moments at curbside: lovers saying goodbye; weary travelers waiting for a pickup; cold transactions between drivers and passengers. Some of my favorite Winogrand photographs capture the low-grade pain of airport waiting: not quite acute, but working on the minds and hearts of these ordinary travelers as the golden age of flight slumps into a routine. The magic of Winogrand's arrivals and departures is how each snapshot seems to arrest a recognizable moment plucked from the relentlessly passing diorama of air travel.

There are the two women with gaggle of children, everyone looking off in a different direction, one child wearing a shirt that says GOODBYE on its back. Their luggage looks unbearably heavy, and they've not even fully crossed the threshold of the curbside.

A bespectacled woman poking her head out of a Mercedes sunroof, mouth agape and staring toward the sliding doors—waiting for someone who, in the seized frame of the photograph, will never arrive.

Airport and airline workers bustling to their appointed positions, heads down, the spectacle of flight long since having been diminished for these exhausted souls.

There's the wind-swept businessman in a three-piece light suit standing behind a yawning car trunk, dark luggage ready to be hauled into the busy transit zone (see Figure 1). He's shielding his eyes from the glaring sun and looking back from whence he came, as if trying to find a point of orientation, or to decipher what propelled him to this spot he is now in, on the ragged seam between ground and air. The horizon is tilted, the airport approach roads arcing dizzyingly away. A sign floats in the top center of the picture, quietly but insistently announcing, "ALL OTHER AIRLINES." There is something transcendent happening in this space—and something vaguely crushing, too.

As portentous and profound as these curbside moments can appear, such scenes are so much more plentiful and plain

Figure 1 © *The Estate of Garry Winogrand, courtesy Fraenkel Gallery, San Francisco.*

than even Winogrand's photos belie. The curbside is a spot of constant transition, cars speeding up and dropping off, or idling in the seconds of rushed farewells, half-anxious hugs. Sometimes checked baggage operations leak out onto the curb, creating an awkward, exhaust-fumed zone where the sheen of travel tarnishes swiftly. The airplane can feel impossibly far away when you're stuck on the curbside.

Here is an exercise to test your tolerance of the curbside: the next time you go to catch a flight, build in an extra ten minutes to spare. Just ten minutes. When your ride drops you off, don't head straight inside. Instead, pause and linger in this space. Can you stay for the entire ten minutes? You may find the suspense of travel too much, and you'll charge inside after only a minute or two. You may find the brutalist architecture of the curbside stifling and oppressive, and bolt within even the first thirty seconds. Or you may just experience a nagging sense of boredom that drives you inside after a few minutes, where no less boredom awaits. What do you observe, though, if you remain?

There is a poetics to the curbside. The curbside is the final line of one stanza, and the opening line of another. It is the last few seconds of being at home, and the first few seconds of being on your way to someplace else. There are quite divergent ways to be in this in-between space: You can dance across the curbside with style and panache, one tightly packed carry-on as your graceful attendant; or you may stumble across, shoelaces untied and jacket flapping, pulling resistant luggage that scrapes against the concrete, wheels invariably jammed.

The curbside can also anticipate the trip to come. It can set everything into disastrous motion, from a hurried goodbye to a botched kiss; or it can initiate a feeling of uplift, of endless possibility as if underlined by the sounds of powerful jet thrusts above.

Airportness gathers and congeals at the curbside—this is truly the *port* of the airport, where you step from one surface onto another, prepared to embark. Or, conversely, it is the last place you touch that you call the airport, once you have arrived. Can this threshold be enhanced, when thinking about airport improvements? And if so, should it be? How and in what ways? Or perhaps we should leave the curbside alone, let it remain as a frayed edge of the nature of flight.

Boarding Pass

Do you remember when we used to get our boarding passes at the airport? We would line up, present IDs and itineraries or receipts, receive cardstock boarding passes and airport navigation tips, and be greeted with a smile or perhaps the distracted gaze of corporate exchange. Of course this space of transaction is still possible—we *can* still check in at the airport, but usually we get a flimsy piece of paper these days, no more magnetic strip on the backside, no more color-coded boarding passes hinting at our net worth. But these days we don't have to go through the ritual any longer. If we are not checking luggage, we can avoid this area of the airport altogether.

For instance, I checked in to my flight today by using my iPhone yesterday, and received my boarding passes right on my screen, now saved in a virtual wallet of sorts. So after I leave the curbside I can orient myself within the terminal, consult a mishmash of bright signs, and head straight to the security line.

I glance over at the check-in lines and see passengers fiddling with papers, looking anxious, hauling oversize bags, and deploying credit cards to pay exorbitant checked baggage fees. The check-in counters are understaffed, and an airline representative is directing people to the self-check-in kiosks. These once forward-moving creatures are suddenly rendered defeated passengers, tapping at cheery screens uncertainly, paper coupons spitting out below. Self-check-in zones often remind me of a sad, short rendition of the film *The Matrix*: on the cusp of unbridled self-mobility, you run into a maddening system.

Not that the new media form of checking in is any less bizarre: getting my boarding passes via the phone is also a displacing experience. It brings the airport home, or to wherever I am when I pull up the check-in screen and go through all the usual procedures. Checking bags? No. Carrying any dangerous items? No. Change seats? Maybe, let's see what's available. Upgrade to first class for $249? Not today, thanks. Now I have two simulacral boarding passes ready at the swipe of my thumb for security personnel and airline agents to consult—or, more accurately, for them to tell me to place my phone face down on a glowing green reader which scans a purchase code, granting me access. The whole procedure is more smooth and sterile than ever, when it works. When it doesn't work, things can get awkward and stressful—fast.

Sometimes I find old boarding passes in books, where I've used them to mark pages or where I shoved them absentmindedly on journeys of the past. Since I have saved time by skipping the check-in counters, let me tell you about an interesting one I've kept all these years: it's a blue United boarding pass from 2006, and on the backside is an advertisement for Nationwide Investments, Retirement, and Insurance (see Figure 2).

This ad plays with the look of safety briefing cards in the seatback pockets of airplanes. In this case, three frames offer instructions for "What to do when you find out your portfolio is packed with a golden parachute." It's *almost* like how to

Figure 2 *Backside of United Airlines ticket stock, 2006.*

escape from a crashed airplane, which safety briefing cards offer instructions for, among other things. This is unnerving, when you think about it: using the metaphor of a parachute—emergency equipment—on a piece of humdrum airline paraphernalia. Who is this humor for? For vulnerable fliers susceptible to fear-based marketing, or for the irony-soaked business travelers of hyper-capitalism?

The informational cartoon begins at the check-in counter, moves to first class seating and zooms in to show the passenger contemplating luxury options, and ends with a "toast to your future." The ad narrates the thoughts of a white, blond-haired male passenger who upgrades to first class, sits in the plane and contemplates various second homes ("Say to self, lake house? Ski house? Lake house? Ski house?"), and then orders a bottle of "the airline's finest champagne" and enjoys a glass alone—all of the other first class seats are unoccupied.

This is classic airportness, wrapping a piece of the journey in more of itself. This ad presumably appeared on every United boarding pass for some time, not *only* on first class ticket stubs.

In those days the first class stubs were colored silver or gold—one was for business class, I can't remember which—and economy class boarding passes came in pale, sickly blue. In other words, the company Nationwide is selling an image of opulence to a necessary substructure of economy: the wish image of solipsistic first class existence is always at the expense of millions of coach class passengers staring at the false promise of a better future. Airportness depends on class-consciousness. The high-flying status of elite travelers necessitates that many, many people lack regular, reliable mobility—not just the dozens of seats in the back of the plane, but even the ride to the airport is out of reach for many, in this schema.

These United Airlines boarding passes were computer generated for every passenger during the time the ad ran, and yet the message of upgrading to first class (metaphorically as well as literally) is exclusivity and uniqueness. Nationwide was promoting white, blond, male self-promotion on a ubiquitous surface, to all passengers. On closer inspection the figure is even more unsettling: his skin is orange, and his hair an unnaturally bleached blond. It is almost as if this advertisement anticipated the rogue popularity of Donald Trump and his rise to power: it is a mixed message of racial superiority and populism, all naturalized under the rubric of airportness.

On the top of the advertisement is the intuitively accurate saying, "Life comes at you fast." Sometimes at the airport, though, this is not the case at all—witness the long mechanical delay. But as shill for insurance it's smart, and it does harken back to the old mid-century scheme of selling life insurance at the airport, where death and disaster were still fresh on fliers' minds. By 2006 the icy threat of imminent terror in the air was thawing, and passengers could be redirected to thinking about their savings, retirement, and luxury items once again.

Another thing that has always struck me about this ad is how the entire airport experience is recreated in miniature on the back of the boarding pass. The passenger/reader is able to interpret airportness by the merest iconography of a ticket agent and then standard (if wide, definitely first class) airliner seats. The whole ensemble of airport experiences is funneled through this simple informational cartoon—and this includes the attendant promises of late modernity (wealth, independence, self-satisfaction, etc.). There is even a petite boarding pass in the first frame, being held up by the ticket agent. This makes the entire cartoon a sort of self-referential art piece, almost a mise en abyme in the form of a minimalist graphic novel. The whole thing conspires to suggest that the world is in the passenger's hand—the hand of that one blond passenger, the hand of an imagined tiny flier on the miniscule boarding pass in the cartoon, and of course in *my* hand as I hustled to my gate somewhere back in 2006.

Around the same time, a friend sent me a bottle of wine from a winery called "Boarding Pass": the logo looks like a boarding pass, and there is a witty baggage tag around the screw top, using an airport code, AUS (the wine is a shiraz from Australia). This is clever marketing that merges travel aesthetics with wine connoisseurship. It also relies on airportness, the familiar memes of commercial flight (see Figure 3).

Figure 3 *Boarding Pass Shiraz.*

The advertising space capitalized on by Nationwide, and the boarding pass motif as displayed on the wine bottle, has ten years later been practically outmoded by the slick efficiencies of our smartphones. Advertising and marketing appear differently, on the screens of our phones. But as we will see, this is fine for airportness, which adapts over time—this too is the nature of flight.

We still need boarding passes, even as they have migrated to our phone screens. And we still need the iconography of boarding passes, on things like wine bottles—we need the idea of the boarding pass, the material object that will grant us permission to go wherever we'd like. But as biometric technologies advance, or, conversely, as air travel becomes less sustainable on a global scale, one wonders about the fate of boarding passes.

Onward now, though, to the melee of the security checkpoint.

Security

I prepare to stand legs apart, arms over my head, in an absurd position reminiscent of elementary physical education drills. We call this progress.

Have you ever stood in a long snaking line, exchanging embarrassed smiles with passengers as you pass them again and again as the line makes its way toward the checkpoint? Have you ever been singled out and "randomly" screened? Have you had something inappropriate happen to you, but been unsure of possible recourse or too flustered or rushed along to do anything about it?

If airport security checkpoints are ground zeros for vulnerability and safety protocols, they are also epicenters of embarrassment, stress, and insecurity. They are the necessary foils of airports, the rude counterbalances to all the progress and uplift of travel. It would be nice to think that security is an anomalous blip within the broader orchestra of airportness, but I suspect that similar paradoxes spill out everywhere and spread in this messy thing we call flight.

Airport security has become something more than a travesty: it has become unremarkable. Don DeLillo has taken note of this, as we can see in a passage from his most recent novel, *Zero K*:

> Those blanked-out eternities at the airport. Getting there, waiting there, standing shoeless in long lines. Think about it. We take off our shoes and remove our metal objects and then enter a stall and raise our arms and get body-scanned and sprayed with radiation and reduced to nakedness on a screen somewhere and then how totally helpless we are all over again as we wait on the tarmac, belted in, our plane eighteenth in line, and it's all ordinary, it's routine, we make ourselves forget it. (172)

The thing about airport security is that it wants the impossible. I remember when I was learning to guide rafts down the Snake

River in Wyoming, and one of the guides training me said, "Never tell a guest that what we're doing is 'safe.'" The point was, going down a swift current river with large jagged rocks everywhere is not safe, ever—even if you make it through intact and everyone has a good time. Even when you try to make sure everyone on the raft is as safe as possible. It's still, fundamentally, *dangerous.* That's part of the draw, no doubt, and what we were paid to help navigate. But it wasn't safe.

And neither is flight. It's a risk to be up there, reliant on countless tiny parts working in concert to make the metal tube actually fly 50 or 100 or 200 humans shaking ever so slightly in their seats. There is nothing secure about this experience.

It is ironic that the serious space of the security checkpoint has become such a site of offhand derision and parody. Louis C. K. does a sketch on it here; *Saturday Night Live* does a skit on it there. This zone that involves so much energy focused on securitization becomes rife with possibilities for sneering and impatience. The security checkpoint consolidates the slipperiness of airportness, how it can flip so easily from one interpretive valence to another. For instance, a recent, earnest advertisement for TSA Pre-check cannot help but end up looking like a joke (see Figure 4).

Two business professionals amble through the airport, apparently having bypassed the security lines using TSA Pre-check. But into what as-if romantic landscape are these postmodern travelers venturing? The shoulder strap of the man's briefcase dangles laughably, and the woman's roller bag is almost sure to not fit the overhead bin, if there's any room left by the time she boards. The space around them is soul-crushingly spare and

Figure 4 *TSA Pre ✓ advertisement at moble.nytimes.com, 2016.*

plain, sunlight glaring off the over-polished floor. It's the opposite of a fecund vacation-scape, and yet here it is urging travelers to fly.

The inner space of this ad appears to be a world of tidy dealings and pressed seams. Uncrowded, unrushed. As opposed, one assumes, to the messy dealings of the security line, where one is inspected and treated roughly for several miserable minutes (or more). "Fewer hassles and less stress" the ad reads, rather redundantly. But as in a work of literary apophasis, wherein the thing claimed to be not said ends up stated anyway, the ad reminds travelers of *all* the hassles and stresses of flight, even as it wishes simply for "a smarter travel experience." The pre-checked travelers nonetheless must march, ever onward and in frozen form, as if on some latter-day Grecian Urn, into the airport.

Even as I wind my way to the checkpoint, my phone dings and an email news alert warns me that security lines will not get shorter anytime soon. This seems like a secure prediction, as the line I'm standing in barely creeps forward. The TSA agents look haggard and weary, waving passengers forward with limp wrists. The entire security team looks stressed out and tired—and it's still early. The once bright blues of their shirts do not match anymore, if they ever did. The machines beep and rumble, and there is the occasional snap as a TSA worker begins her or his shift and pulls on a fresh pair of blue latex gloves. The conveyor belt sucks bags into the x-ray chamber, and human bodies are scanned. This human-and-bag-scanning contraption churns and processes me, pulling me slowly toward its strange center.

Walk to the Gate

We're really in the airport, now. Let's walk together, take it all in.

The first steps past security are always a little rubbery. Some passengers are still dragging belts or jackets, or flopping barefoot as they look for a seat where they can re-comport themselves. Some people head to the nearest food kiosk to buy something, as if to reclaim their independence after having been thoroughly scanned and frisked.

What is this walk, this walk that is oriented toward a gate number or letter-number sequence, like some elementary school activity repurposed for the supposed pinnacle of adult life? This walk is all but forgotten, most of the time. We are either in a hurry, shaken from the security scrum, or simply numb to this obligatory amble.

Far out in the American West, on the Pacific coast, lies an airport where such terminal walking has been targeted as something to be eliminated. As a *Guardian* headline from 2015 read, "Los Angeles airport to build special terminal just for celebrities." The article reports:

> Welcome to the 1%'s new airport terminal. Los Angeles international airport [recently] won approval to build a special terminal to allow celebrities, sports stars and the world's wealthy to glide directly from their chauffeur-driven limo to their first-class seat without having to interact with any of the general travelling public.

Here is an astonishingly cynical vision of airportness, one that essentially seeks to "build a wall," to adopt an unfortunately popular saying, such that the elite do not have to mingle with common folk. The pragmatic goal is to avoid the sort of "media scrums" that can happen when ordinary passengers see a celebrity in the airport—or when paparazzi explicitly target celebrity sightings at convenient congestion points. I'm sure you are familiar with such scenes.

I once stumbled upon an unpleasant yet fascinating YouTube video that captured the singer Björk in 1996 trundling her luggage through the nether regions of the Bangkok airport, through a gauntlet of paparazzi and nagging journalists, only to suddenly lose it and hurl herself on a woman holding out a microphone. The frame shakes, and hair and clothes seem to be caught in a whirlwind on the hard terminal floor. The fluorescent lights beat down on the scuffle; finally, someone drags Björk off the tousled journalist, and the group moves away, everyone looking slightly aghast and shaken.

Björk was shamed for losing her temper and resorting to violence, and indeed by all accounts it was an unwarranted physical attack. However, the singer later claimed that this particular journalist had been hounding her for days, pestering the singer and her son relentlessly with probing personal questions, shouted at high volume wherever Björk went—and therefore she understandably, finally, lost her temper. Björk had apparently requested no media be at the airport when she arrived, and instead the press bombarded her when she passed through customs, walking a familiar walk, that democratic trudge from the gate.

So the new LAX celebrity terminal would seem, on one level, a simple strategic move to avoid such unpleasant confrontations. This sounds innocent enough. But curiosities abound within the reporting of this new celebrity terminal, including the detail that the "new airport"—which sounds at first like a grand building project—will in fact be located in an old hangar building. The experience is intended to be entirely interior, invisible from the public eye. If nature loves to hide, as the Greek philosopher Heraclitus once supposed, wealth likes to hide even more, these days.

And this compression or disappearing of the journey is not only an inside/outside matter. Within the celebrity terminal, foot travel will be reduced to a bare minimum, such that a familiar, presumably *healthy* airport ritual—mere walking—is all but eliminated. As the *Guardian* article reports: "The plans promise that guests using the new terminal will have to walk about 60 steps, compared to as many as 2,200 from street to plane seat via the public terminals." In this bizarre post-Western fantasy, the new frontiersman becomes less dependent on humanoid appendages. Bodily adventure is something to be *avoided*. And then, in the immortal words of the singer-songwriter Neko Case, "Heaven will smell like the airport."

Lest this seem like a Los Angeles anomaly, the *Guardian* article reports that there are also "plans to introduce similar facilities at New York's JFK and possibly San Francisco, Miami, Chicago and Dallas." In the future, then, we may differentiate between stupid, sweating, *walking* air travelers, and those sheltered behind limousines, swept into drab hangar spaces whose illustrious innards we might fancy ... but never touch, or if so, only to displace one of the elite members and send them back to groveling, pedestrian existence.

David Bowie was onto something when he sang, not without some irony, "Fame: what you want is in the limo." The LAX celebrity terminal is an inverted American fantasy, where instead of the great outdoors, people are lured by the promise of total privilege: a sealed off form of existence—no exposure, no contact, no hassle. Airportness persists here only as a minimal trace, a shell of itself. It is the apotheosis of the first class/ economy division: a decisive separation that readily admits that some people are simply worth more than hordes of others. We shouldn't pursue a path that would "Make Airports Great Again," if this is what we mean by such a slogan. For then, we would have to believe that the airport can and should be avoided at all costs, and that the truly great airport is actually the one you never see, or never set foot into. This contradicts actually making airports better, or changing for the better how we inhabit them.

When we hear calls for airport improvements, they often sound like appeals to abstract, mythical, heavenly airports—airports not unlike the LAX celebrity terminal. We don't need these sorts of airports. We could use nicer airports, perhaps—but nicer in spirit and action, not just in terms of cordoned off spaces and minimal walking. The future airport might yet shrink walking distances, but let's not segregate and seclude people along the way. For down this path lie the sorts of bitter divisions and animosity that do not bode well for global coexistence. Let's go somewhere else, somewhere better—to an airport to come, where all people will be invited, and none treated unfairly. Is this too much to ask for?

For now, the future airport is not our airport. We still have a bit of a walk ahead of us before we get to our gate.

People Watching

People watching at airports is something not to be missed or forgotten. People from everywhere, donning all manner of clothes and habits, pass through these spaces. As the poet Brenda Hillman observes, "It's hardly apparent who will travel" ("Symmetry Breaking" 1997: 54). But of all these people at the airport, while most are travelers, many are workers. Find yourself a sling seat, try to be as inconspicuous as possible—and just watch for an hour. If you pay attention, you will see countless acts of care, assistance, and kind interactions in bloom throughout the hustle and bustle of flight. Consider airports as microcosms of a culture—perhaps even the human world—and they might be models of cooperation, collaboration, and communication.

Of course airports aren't always like this. A lot of times they are "nasty" places, in the parlance. People are rushing headlong, dragging screaming children. Some travelers appear lost, panicked. Others angrily bark into their phones as they yank their roller bags. Airline employees snap at passengers, or get reamed out themselves for things beyond their control. Remember that airports are the people, not simply the structures surrounding them. Buildings can be improved and elegantly adorned, but it is the people who matter.

Before we set out to overhaul these spaces, let's not forget to observe the people. All of the people. Take the time to watch people: this is us, not just Americans at American airports, but humans trembling on delicate lines of transit everywhere around the globe.

Attack

Another walk through the concourse, another news alert on the big plasma screens of an airport attack, somewhere. Passengers loiter on the sun-blasted tarmac, jetliners immobile and awkward looking. It's eerie: here we are in the same sort of space and yet most people seem determined to walk on by, to keep going. A few people cluster under the screen, hands to their mouths or scrolling on their phones.

Let's not stop to watch the awful panning shots of a terminal in disarray—these images are too uncanny.

I remember when the *Mirror* posted a particularly clickbaity listicle with the headline "Are Travellers Safe? From Istanbul to Glasgow and Brussels—10 airport attacks that shook the world." The subhead read: "After 41 killed in Turkish airport attack it's clear airport terminals are now the place for terrorists targeting the innocent." The June 2016 attack at the Istanbul airport was atrocious, and stung especially as it came close on the heels of the awful Brussels bombings that March. But the *Mirror*'s notion that airports have only "now" become targets is just plain wrong.

Since their inception, airports have been "the place" for spectacles of violence. It's not always terrorism, though. Sometimes it's a daredevil stunt gone awry, other times it's a terrible crash or near disaster. Occasionally it has to do with the military occupation of these otherwise civilian spaces. Throughout the twentieth century and up to now, airports have been stages for displays of excessive power, and their corollary dangers.

The airport-as-target trope has become so ubiquitous at this point that an entire scene of the blockbuster *Captain America: Civil War* was dedicated to terminal carnage. This scene was then exported and repackaged as a Marvel Super Heroes themed Lego set called "Airport Battle" that features a few stock tarmac objects (an air traffic control tower, a luggage cart and

Tug, wands for ramp agents) to stand for the whole ensemble of an airport. Lego lets you have fun building and then destroying an airport, in miniature.

What makes airports popular targets for violent spectacles?

First theory: Airports are preeminent sites of progress, cosmopolitanism, and freedom. So oppressive regimes and their ilk target these spaces to cause symbolic as well as real damage. However, air travel is so regularly disparaged and frustratingly tolerated in public discourse that this doesn't seem right. Perhaps during the so-called "golden age" of flight, airports loosely held this special place in the public's mind—but definitely not anymore.

So, a second theory: Airports are places where masses of people congregate, thereby making them apt points of congestion and confusion at which to stage an attack. But this theory doesn't hold up: there are plenty of other places in contemporary society that combine masses and modern rituals (stadiums, mega churches, shopping malls, theme parks—"soft targets," as they are called). And while such sites get attacked too, from time to time, they are not frantically guarded like airports are.

This leads to a third theory: Airports are access points to big weapons (airliners) that can be commandeered for nefarious ends. But besides 9/11 and a handful of other hijackings, airplanes have not been the focus of airport attacks. It is usually more about inflicting violence on innocent passengers and random airline workers.

Finally, a fourth theory: The prevalence of airports as sites of drama—delays and cancellations for one, but also crashes, bombings, extreme weather, cinematic action, hijackings, air rage, even toy airport battles—has created a vicious feedback loop: people look to airports for trouble, and they find it there, no matter the political, voyeuristic, or violent agendas.

The last theory is probably the most accurate, if also the most troubling, because it implicates everyone. It means that in order to break this feedback loop, the public would have to radically change travel by air—and not just by adding ever more layers of security. As it is, with new airliners stolidly projected to last at least thirty years, things seem determined to persist basically as they are.

It shouldn't come as a surprise that the status quo for airports is a whole package, all the risks, rewards, and ruins of flight. Airports promise freedom but deliver discomfort, and that makes them suitable venues for attacks. And then these spectacles are subsumed back into the ordinary grind of travel, on the airport TV channel and further still onto entertainment screens everywhere. Television has been a key ingredient to the fame and power of the new American president. Likewise, when thinking about airports, media streams are far from neutral features within and beyond our terminal landscapes.

Waiting

Airport waiting is the occupation of an awkward temporality. Relatively concentrated and constrained by a constantly moving structure (inbound and outbound flights), this time can veer uncomfortably in an instant. It can also sink in and feel terribly protracted. Passengers work hard to annihilate this time—or they merely tune out, stare off into space.

Where I am sitting now, I feel the whole giant airport shaking beneath me, a low-frequency hum and a palpable vibration rattling my seat. A bottled water near me evinces the rumble, water lapping gently at the inner walls of the plastic container. Enormous jets roll slowly past on the tarmac outside, muffled and graceful. Sparrows flit near me, gathering crumbs from the carpet.

While it is a field day for quiet observation, not many have the patience for this—and it is impolite to be caught staring, even though so many costumes on display scream to be stared at. From the sexed-up to the sweatpanted, from the strung-out rock star look to the frazzled family unit taking up the entire hallway—it is all happening at the airport, all waiting to be seen and . . . if not appreciated, exactly, at least be taken note of. Human forms bustle around the slapdash improvisations of construction and renovation, and they cluster around chintzy pop-up stands between gates.

On pause between day-to-day life and the terrific transition across the sky, airport waiting exposes us in a way almost too uncomfortable to discuss openly. We can mitigate this time with overlarge beers or engorgements of sugar; we can zone out to the droning tones of airport TV. Airportness is the palliative agent and the poison here: it's the creepy feeling that makes our skin crawl, and the panoply of options that promise to make the time disappear.

But no matter what we do or how we pass this time in the airport, here we are, waiting for our lives to restart, as if we never learned the meaning of the present. Is this what we're like in the country at large right now, waiting for something better? Should we perhaps look around a bit more, appreciate what we have, what we've accomplished? Then, only then, might we actually get better. It isn't all about airports. It's about how we treat people, how we treat time and space. This sounds impossibly grandiose, possibly—but we've got a big trip ahead of us, and airports are just one part, themselves spiraling inward and sprawling outward.

Workers

Look around us, at all the workers.

One of my favorite children's books about air travel, *Planes*, by Byron Barton, includes two pages late in the book that read: "These are workers / cleaning and checking" (21–22). Busy workers of many colors and genders move around the plane that has just landed, preparing it for its next flight. I love the directness of this sequence, and the simple lesson: airport work is hard work, diverse work—and it's ongoing. Eight hours of loading luggage or standing behind a boarding gate is no easy feat. As we continue through the airport, let's keep this in mind: a lot of people work here, and their lives matter as much as the passengers' trajectories. When we talk about improving airports, we may think first of smoother logistics and more opulent amenities for travelers—the "customer experience"—but airports are also workplaces, and this fact should not be forgotten.

When I teach my airport class, I have a final assignment where the students have to go spend four hours at an airport— our local Louis Armstrong airport, or sometimes students do this at their home airports when they are home for vacation. Either way, I ask them to spend at least four hours observing, wandering around, and documenting what they see. Their final presentations involve showing the rest of the class what they learned by lingering at the airport. They often notice the workers, and all the work going on that they'd never taken note of before. So one lesson in my class (and for this book as well) is that airportness is not just the built space, and not just the phenomenology of the passenger, but also the workers and the working conditions that make these places what they are. Remember the wisdom of Byron Barton: "These are workers / cleaning and checking."

Art

Walking further down the concourse, what do we see? We may glance disinterestedly at a series of abstract watercolor paintings adorning the wall. Of course, it is hardly a stark gallery space, interrupted as it is by tawdry ads for a burrito shack in the C concourse, wine tasting adventures in the newest best vineyard in this part of the country, the latest sprightly roller bag available, and noise-cancelling headphones. Still, the humble watercolors do their thing, insinuating "art" in the mayhem of the airport.

Somewhere between commercial and conceptual art, airport art often tries to be provocatively—sometimes cloyingly—thematic. Historic aviation photography, or flight-themed sculptures that use luggage, propellers, or other plane parts to conjure the feelings of air travel. Other airport art veers toward the milquetoast, regional variety, with sweeping panoramic views of plains, or murals that echo the views beyond the tarmac. Still other airport art goes for local sentiment. I recall once seeing a charming display of drawings by schoolchildren lining the long walk to the baggage claim in the Portland, Oregon, airport.

My home airport in New Orleans has some enigmatic artwork in the B concourse, near the Lucky Dog stand. They are large paintings of the views out airliner windows, blatantly aestheticizing ubiquitous views above the clouds from the vantage point of a regular passenger staring out. They are recognizable, and realistic—if also slightly out of context. For at this point, we're not yet in the air or on the airplane, but we're close to these things. Ready to fly, but currently putting up with all the annoyances of airport life: expensive bottled water, cacophonous background noise, and shrill announcements that are nevertheless unintelligible.

But these paintings suggest something else. Turning window seat views into art and then placing them at the airport seem to demand something extra from the experience at hand. Like: *This is art! You are part of an elaborate artwork! Appreciate it!* These demands ring hollow, of course, when gate changes and temperamental computer systems rule the day. But consider this, next time you are in the airport or in the airplane, is this, too, an elaborate work of art? What would it mean to embrace airports as art?

Gate Change

Busy contemplating the role of art in airports, and airports as art, I miss a notification on my phone. There has been a gate change, and we need to huff it to the other end of the concourse, where our (new) plane is now preparing to board.

Isn't it funny how you can see one plane out the window, projecting a kind of abstract ownership of it, a sense that *that* plane will take you to your destination, when it can so suddenly become just another plane waiting for other people, and *your* plane is now somewhere else across the airport? Of course this kind of switcheroo is routine here, another feature of airportness that orients you just as it disorients you. This is your gate. This is no longer your gate. Say "gate" twenty times fast and see if it still means the same thing when you're done.

Sometimes gate changes can spiral into cataclysmic cancellation fests, where ten gate changes end in a bleak sign that says "CANCELLED." Other times, like now, thankfully, it is a mere single gate change that, as I can see as we approach our new gate, will result in a smooth transition, and everyone pretends that nothing happened, as if this was our plane after all, the whole time.

When we reach the gate, the gate agent is just announcing the boarding order: a staggering hierarchy of loyalty levels and elitisms, soon to be funneled into the tinny jet bridge.

Gate Lice

Have you ever had lice? What about gate lice? Gate lice are passengers who flock and linger near the departure gate, before proper boarding has commenced. They inch closer to the podium or entrance to the jet bridge; they eavesdrop on the airline gate agents or absently thumb their phones. They lean against their roller bags and sometimes crouch or kneel, as if ready to spring forth when they are called to board. Maybe the gate change has made it worse than normal, but as we approach, I see dozens of them, hovering.

Let's take a seat across the concourse, a vantage point from which we can observe the gate lice without becoming part of them.

Eye contact is usually avoided among gate lice, unless there is a delay or cancellation announcement, and then they may team up, clustering together and forming sudden alliances. Gate lice often smell like hotel soap, and occasionally wear special shoes with extra arch support. I'll bet that "Untuckit" shirt company thrives on purchases from gate lice; these are button-down shirts cleverly tailored to be left un-tucked, relentlessly advertised in the pages of in-flight magazines. Gate lice do not self-identify as gate lice, but rather think of themselves as lone wolves (to mix metaphors slightly)—even as their collective behavior at times suggests a pack mentality. Gate lice are an indicator species, a sign of the inefficiencies of airport space and time, one of our most prized, made ecosystems. Gate lice are yet another feature of airportness, recognizable creatures that communicate that a flight is about to board.

Once you start focusing on gate lice, you will not want to be one—you will want to distance yourself from their drifting presence. Inevitably, though, we all become gate lice. Even now, as I write this furtively from across the hall, tucked into the opposite gate area, I feel myself pulled into their shifting mass as boarding time nears. I calculate and consider the swarm, not wanting to get too far behind in the boarding queue. Eventually I am there with them, I am moving with them, I am gate lice, my toes clutching the airport carpet and inching toward the airplane. To rephrase Walt Whitman, from "Song of Myself," I am "the mate and companion of" gate lice (37). Airportness is how we move together as a species, in ways that can be repugnant once we become aware of them, and shameful to admit.

Fishing Shirts

Just as baseball caps are no longer exclusively for baseball (cf. "Make America Great Again"), fishing shirts are not just for fishing anymore. Or maybe they never were. Every time my friend Ian is at the airport, it seems he is surrounded by passengers wearing fishing shirts. He often snaps a picture of an unsuspecting adventurer and sends it to me, as a kind of inside joke. One time Ian became unnerved, *Matrix*-style, when he noticed that the Delta gate agent, too, was wearing an airline-branded fishing shirt. It was as if the symbolic structure had collapsed, as if leisure and labor had finally merged into the same uniform.

Surprisingly, these garments have come to reek of airportness, framed as they are by the monotonous details of boarding gates and shoulder slung computer bags. And now as we march down the jet bridge I notice not one, not two, but *three* fishing shirts in line with us, two in front and one just behind me. I am tempted to snap a picture and send it to Ian, but I'd have to use the panoramic function on my phone, and it would be awkward to say the least. Plus, the line is moving and we're all itching to get into our seats. Still, the fishing shirts flash at me, taunting, with their poly-cotton blends and their articulated vents catching the fluorescent light beaming down from the jet bridge ceiling.

What are these things that would seem dissonant with airport life and yet have come to define it in their own small way? Fishing shirts are a modified version of the travel shirt, a many-pocketed button-down shirt that looks somewhat like an Oxford-cloth business casual staple, until you get up close—then you see the details: vent flaps, mesh linings, patch pockets with accordion folds and pleats, key loops, utility tabs, expandable collars for sun protection . . . the list goes on. What do these shirts offer, whence their popularity, beyond the conceit of actual fishing? And how might they be another piece of airportness?

Look around next time you are at the airport, and observe the drab drapings of these high-tech shirts as they make contact with plastic seats and press against plate glass windows. Behold the arm of a fellow traveler hauling a roller bag down the jet bridge—the flexed arm sleeved within a gusseted fishing shirt. Then consider how these shirts are robustly described by their purveyors.

The Columbia PFG (Performance Fishing Gear) "Tamiami II," probably the most common and eerily identifiable fishing shirt (you may not even know you know it, but you probably do), offers a "Modern Classic fit" and is "designed for cool comfort and functionality over the long haul." The "cool" does double duty, assuring us that we will look fashionable while also evincing the functional venting technology of this shirt. The "long haul" cannot help but connote flight. No wonder it is called a "performance button up," as it must skate an awkward path between the noble pursuits of modernity and the banal realities of endless office work. When Ian saw the Delta workers wearing Columbia PFG shirts emblazoned with the airline's logo, there was something disturbing about this—as if some weird collapse between passenger and airline worker had occurred, and perhaps between labor and leisure.

Patagonia's "Island Hopper II" promises "a superlight long-sleeved shirt in an easy-care, organic cotton, recycled polyester blend." Consider here the tension between "easy-care" and the implied responsibilities of *organic* cotton and *recycling*: environmental consciousness dances on a razor's edge between calm and crisis. An "island hopper" is a kind of plane, too, suggesting escapades in the seas, with the ability to jump from one landmass to another at will.

Meanwhile, ExOfficio's "Air Strip™ Shirt" is marketed as "the ultimate in technical apparel." At the same time, it assures a "comfortable yet modern silhouette"—by now a familiar formula, this vow to balance utility with elegance. It's also an *airstrip*—metaphoric planes are landing on your sleeve, or taking off. Airborne logistics are woven into the seams.

And isn't this what is so attractive—and so galling—about a fishing shirt at the airport? It pledges to spirit us through the world with foresight, durability, and protection; but it also nestles blandly into the consumerscape numbly taking place all around. It beckons at trout unlimited and adventures untold; and it seamlessly facilitates herds of shuffling travelers and routine labor. It's everything about modernity we'd wanted—packaged in all sizes and colors, and made for every occasion. Airportness dilutes our traveling inclinations, even as it increases them a thousandfold. With the democratization of flight comes the banalization of adventure. Why teach anyone to fish, when everyone can just wear a fishing shirt?

I look down as I cross the threshold of the jet bridge and step onto the plane, over that brief seam of air and outside light. And then I shudder, realizing something: I am wearing a variation of a fishing shirt, myself.

Runway

As boarding continues, and as we prepare to taxi out to the runway, I look out over this familiar landscape, shrouded in darkness yet spotlighted severely in places. The runway is a field of planes, a matrix of vectors—as evinced by the skid marks from the tires on touchdown that scar the two ends of the gray strip. How do you feel about runways? Do you get anxious, jittery? Or do you feel an adrenaline rush as the engines thrum? Do you see everything happening out there, or do you block it out, focused on matters beyond?

David Foster Wallace, in his first novel *The Broom of the System*, describes a runway scene aptly:

> A bright day, in very early September, everything dry, the sun an explicit thing, up there, with heat coming right off it, but a flat edge of cool running down the middle of the day. A jet airplane stood at lunchtime on Runway 1 at CHA, pointed west to go east, a red-ink drawing of a laughing baby on its side, guys with earmuffs and orange plastic flags torn at by the wind off the flatness taking iron prisms out from under the airplane's wheels, the air behind the engines hot and melting the pale green fields through it, the engines hissing through the dry wind like torches, fuel-shimmers. The guys slowly waving the orange flags. The sun glinting off the slanted glass of the windshield, behind which there are sunglasses and thumbs-ups. One of the flag-guys is wearing a Walkman, instead of earmuffs, and he twirls with his flag. (179)

This passage uses a seemingly tangential airport scene as a neutral setting, and it also reflects a certain *reading* of this space: it is atmospheric, satirical, theatrical, and imagistic. Since we have time as boarding continues, linger on this paragraph with me, taking it one sentence at a time, while we're still on the ground. "Airplane reading" will become a theme in this book, a way of passing time and looking closely at the forms of life entangled in airportness.

Back to the text: Wallace's first sentence establishes a mixed feeling, of the scorching sun offset by an inviting autumn zephyr. In the next sentence the airliner protrudes, standing still "at lunchtime"—lending the jet animacy, its own cravings. (Or this might simply remind us of the consumptive aura of modernity, more generally.) The next sentence is long and very busy, a classic bit of Wallace: "Runway 1" is an utterly vague denotation, yet at the same time connotatively powerful; CHA a misnomer (given the novel's geography Wallace likely meant Cleveland Hopkins airport but that would be CLE; CHA is Chattanooga; never mind, it's fiction); "pointed west to go east" suggests the necessary loops involved in the circuits of technoculture; the laughing baby livery a satire of hyperbolic cuteness and mandatory happiness; the ramp workers with their tattered flags perform the bare life of airport labor, pulling chocks from landing gear while exposed in the "melting" air; humans, roaring plane, and landscape merge in this sentence into a fiery shimmer, a collapse of nature and culture, a swarming of senses, affects, and objects. The slowly waved orange flags operate as esoteric semaphores, suggesting a carefully choreographed (if also worn out) performance in process. Mediated behind the glinting glass of the cockpit we glimpse the pilots via synecdoches of "sunglasses and thumbs-up"—these are not pilots, these are pilot-functions, people stripped down to their rote roles within this mundane (and maybe horrifying) machine. And yet one ramp worker's previously noted earmuffs turn out to be headphones, presumably blasting a stream of private entertainment into the guy's ears, while the "hissing" commercial maelstrom unfurls all around. Is this a glimmer of individual resistance, even expression? Or is the Walkman a mere corollary to the heavy ensemble, the encompassing regime? Is the airport worker plugged in or tuned out—or is he enacting both comportments at once? The "twirling" of the flag leaves us with a playful uncertainty as to the determinacy and/or frivolity of this entire passage—and maybe with respect to the whole grid of acts and trajectories at work here on the tarmac, and beyond.

Through this striking set of images, Wallace offers a highly condensed meditation on some of the puzzles of the jet age; he shows us how to *read* the runway. This is airportness, nestled into a passing paragraph within the larger movements of the novel. Incidentally, concerning airports, Wallace wrote in his final, unfinished novel *The Pale King*, "Not every path is outlined in neon lights like an airport runway" (158). Runways are at once clear and murky things, seeming to be a straight path, but maybe also more and less than this.

Our own plane is now being pushed back, and will soon rumble to a stop at the beginning of the runway, ready to take off. But first, the takeaway: runways are not just paved spaces to land and launch airplanes. They are loaded with meaning: they absorb and reflect all our hopes, dreams, and nightmares with respect to human flight. Don't shy away from the complexities of air travel. A runway is always more than a runway: airports extend beyond the tarmac and up into the sky, and deep into our minds.

Holding

We're now in line for takeoff, holding while a bank of inbound planes land. I love to watch the planes come in for landing, seeing their distant lights drop toward the horizon and suddenly materialize into real, live airliners.

Curious about where we've ended up on the big footprint of the airport, I take out my phone and open up the map application, selecting the satellite view of my whereabouts. As the satellite imagery renders, I am confronted with a peculiar sight: the airport wavers as it comes into focus, and for a moment the scene uncannily resembles a Wayne Thiebaud painting. I take a screen grab of it as it wobbles into clarity (see Figure 5).

As I pan over the airport, a smudgy Boeing 747 appears with its signature humpback and dual jet bridges. Somehow, seeing the iconic jumbo jet on my iPhone screen this way makes the plane sublime in a new way, more painterly and objectified. The scene captures the essence of airportness, what with the unused jet bridges nearby, the depthless shadows, the vacant tarmac surrounding the plane, and the bare minimum of the airport concourse in the bottom right-hand corner.

This image sends my mind reeling, thinking once again about the nature of flight that is itself an artwork, a dazzling composition of people, planes, and myriad other things all working together to make each singular flight leave the ground, to eventually return. Satellite imagery of airports shows them in a perpetual state of holding, arresting all the dynamism and

Figure 5 *iPhone Maps satellite imagery.*

motion of flight, and revealing their basic forms and materials. Minus people, at least here, the airport on my iPhone looks like a postapocalyptic background, some vast wasteland long abandoned by whatever animals or machines brought this place into being. I'm captivated by this scene, even as I'm a captive of it in the moment.

The engines rev up, and the plane rolls forward. Let's turn off our phones, shut down Twitter or Instagram for a few moments, at least. We're on the verge of flight; let's savor it.

Takeoff

Who can deny the miraculous feeling of takeoff, when the engine whine increases to a roar, your body is pushed back into the seat, and the whole airport becomes a blur, only then to recede into the distance down below? Do you still feel the extraordinary sensation of takeoff, once it has become so routine to you?

I remember when my son first experienced a takeoff, the look in his wide eyes as the plane vaulted up and angled out over our city. "The cars look like little ants!" he said. He was swept up in the lift, dizzied by the sight out his window. I could see him feeling his body being thrust backward, as if suddenly aware of his very being-there. The view outside, the feeling inside—it was almost too much for him, and I recognized that swirl of sensations.

But I look around me now, and no one seems to notice that we are hurtling down the runway, heading toward that point called "rotation" where the landing gear leaves the Earth and we are, at once, in flight.

This feeling becomes humdrum for the regular traveler, just another moment in the tedious journey from here to there. We barely even register it anymore—except if we are first-time or fearful fliers. For the most part, though, it is as if we are on a bus or any other form of mass transit: we stolidly settle in for the ride, and the takeoff is simply another part of it to be gotten through. I am as guilty of this as anyone: though I still enjoy the rush of takeoff, often I immerse myself in a short story or novel during taxiing and takeoff, to pass the time—especially if I want to avoid chitchat with a gregarious seatmate.

What would it take to recapture the joy of takeoff, on a mass scale? Has the nature of flight become too banal for its own good? When airportness fades into the background, or becomes a tolerated discomfort, have we forgotten something about why we travel in the first place? These questions may seem naïve, but I am sincerely puzzled about this: how something as magical as flight—and especially that moment of release from the ground—can become so profoundly taken for granted. It might be that air travel is just like any other convenience of modernity, with its own gives and takes, but I think flight is different: it's something about where our species is *going*, in more ways than one.

Window Seat

The window seat is a special place. My friend Ian insists that it's a renewable contract to stay seated during the duration of the flight; no one likes a window seatmate who continually gets up to pee. At the window seat you can have a remarkable amount of control over the ambience of the rest of your row, in other ways too: you can darken it or lighten it at your will, given the time of the flight and the angle of the sun. Then there are the views: milky clouds on ascent or descent, distant cumulonimbus stacks, spread-out sunrises, or dessert dripping sunsets. The web has become a vast repository and archive for such vistas, bringing the window seat down to earth, repositioning these views at our desks, on our computers, and in other modes of transit as we stare into and swipe at our smartphone screens. Just type "window seat" into a Google Image search or Flickr, and you'll see what I mean.

But the phenomenology of the airborne window seat is still unique, even as it risks fading into banality. As I write this I am not in a window seat, but instead in an aisle seat—not my preference, but due to some last minute seat jockeying by a couple in my originally assigned row who wanted to sit together, I ended up here. I don't like to make a fuss on planes—no one ever wins.

Because this is an early morning flight, many of the window shades are drawn shut. Mountainous terrain unfurls beneath us—I can see it from my aisle seat from time to time, when the plane banks. But based on the few dozen passengers I can see from my mid-cabin vantage point, no window seat occupants seem to be gazing out at the topography below, or into the cloudscape. There's nothing wrong with this, I suppose, but it does suggest a diminishment of the sublimity once assumed to be a natural experience associated with aerial views.

As I look across three passengers to my left, out the window I see the wing bisecting the view at an angle, pale blue receding into the distance. It's nothing dramatic, but I can still conjure a slight feeling of the window seat sublime. The aura of the window seat view—it is breathtaking, if you let it be. Do you ever find yourself staring out the window, when you're in flight? If not, try it next time. Just stare out at the billowing cloud banks, or at the mountains, suburbs, or sea scrolling below.

Over the years I've seen numerous airline ads that feature a contented passenger lost in reverie, gazing out from the window seat, placid visage caught in a warm glow. This is a nice image, but it's mostly untrue. The vast majority of window seat passengers, such as on this flight, are zoned out, sleeping or glowering at their seatback screens, toggling between popular entertainment and airline fed information. Some passengers watch the satellite view route map, oversize plane icon crawling unhurriedly across the map on the screen. Others use this time to labor, entering data into spreadsheet cells or filling out work reports. The window seat sublime surrounds everyone, but remains largely unseen. It is a prop for airline loyalty programs, a lure and an apparently reliable spectacle—but it is also a ruse. Except for first-time fliers or occasional fanatics, who may spend prolonged minutes staring out at cloud banks ever adjusting their forms.

In a museum bookstore I once picked up a book by Gregory Dicum called *Window Seat: Reading the Landscape from the Air*. This book is essentially about geography and topography, but uses commercial air travel as its framing mechanism—specifically, the perspectives granted by window seats. In the afterword of the book, Dicum writes:

> If you're reading this, it must be cloudy, or nighttime. Or, perhaps you're laid over between flights or your seatmate has insisted that you lower the shade so she can watch that

infernal movie about talking dogs. For whatever reason, you're presently unable to gaze like a heavenly being across the unfolding continent. (168)

Romantic in tone, Dicum's book is an expansive—if visually vertiginous—overview of this particular experience of seeing the world through the windows of flight. But intriguingly, false perspectives riddle the book. Many of the images included in the book seem to be satellite rendered, rather than window seat views; and even the geography lessons that appear throughout the book presume that the window seat always affords a clear, unobstructed view from above. The reality is that even a craned neck rarely achieves such a straight-down perspective. Dicum's wry comment about a seatmate closing the window shade serves as a rude exception—when in fact it is more like the rule.

The window seat sublime is still out there. It is a part of airportness, a part of the journey we recognize and which some of us like to share, from time to time. But you have to take the time to look for it, to really get lost in it. Or, seeing as how so many of us do not want to take the time to look, or do not have an interest in these views—maybe it is time to retire the window seat and all its enabling technologies. Time to seek new forms of sublimity, if not necessarily higher ones.

Sunrise

Sunrises from the vantage point of airliners at cruising altitude can be especially stunning. The sunrise right now is so spectacular that I can see it even though I'm not in a window seat. It turns the cabin interior pink and luminous as the glowing orb rises and illumines the clouds below. Passengers trying to sleep, however, are annoyed by the shifting light beams, and they cover their heads with sweaters or jackets. The smell on board an aircraft at sunrise is *not* especially stunning: the coffee aroma a little off, the stench of early morning sweat or gas wafting between seats.

How do you view the sun when you are in flight? Do you think of it as a far off place, a source of heat and light, or little more than an abstract, regularly occurring presence and absence? Is it something that annoyingly gets in your eyes, or something you take the time to respect and bask in?

The French critic Roland Barthes once contrasted trains and planes in a passage of his eponymous auto-theoretical book:

> On trains, I have ideas: people are moving around me, and the passing bodies act as catalysts. On planes, it is just the contrary: I am motionless, stuck, blind; my body and consequently my intellect are dead: the only thing at my disposal is the movement of the varnished and absent body of the stewardess, circulating like an indifferent mother among the cradles of a day nursery. (*Roland Barthes* 2010: 142)

I recognize this sensation—or this dulling of sensations—that can occur when in flight. Yes, there is a certain mystery to trains that makes planes seem gloomy in comparison. But I want to push back on this intuitive feeling, to try to tune in to the ordinary facts of flight—like the sunlight pouring through the windows and illuminating the interior of this soaring tube.

For me, the sun in this space evokes a sense of planetary awareness, an impression of profound smallness—and when in flight during a sunrise, I find myself entertaining the deep contradiction of feeling like the smartest species, having overcome our own earthbound limitations . . . while at the same time being blinded by our own ascendancy.

Armrests

Amid all the advice columns and cautionary tales about fraught family get-togethers this past Thanksgiving, after the 2016 election, I found myself wondering about another place where people with potentially opposing views find themselves in close quarters: on the airplanes that transported everyone before and after the holidays. It's not only around the dinner table that divergent opinions may emerge and lead to confrontations. In many ways the cabins of commercial airliners can be even more intense, what with the cramped interiors, limited personal space, and short tempers at play. I'm feeling this right now as I have a very subdued, unspoken negotiation with my seatmate, as we each try to achieve a smidgen of elbow support from the thin bar between us. We each hope the other won't snap as we adjust and fit into our seats, embodied pieces of a surreal puzzle.

One of my favorite recent stories by Lydia Davis is called "The Woman Next to Me on the Airplane." I don't even need to summarize the very short piece of fiction—the title pretty much says it all. Airplane rows commonly have two or three seats to a row, and even though passengers are assigned their own discrete spaces—14D, 14E, 14F, for instance—it's really more like sharing a bench with slim dividers between each person. It's actually a minor miracle that air travel this past Thanksgiving didn't turn into a total meltdown, given the volatile crosscurrents of hostility, anger, sadness, and pride swirling around the postelection United States. What if airliners are where we are at our best, not *despite* but *because of* the tight quarters? In this moment of national division and uncertainty about the future, let's pause to think about these things a little more.

Armrests in commercial airliners are strange things. When you board the plane, the armrests are usually raised, nestled in between the seats. If you are the first to sit in your row, you may slide an armrest down, to demarcate your space or just to settle in. Or, you may leave it up, hoping that no one sits next to you—in which case you can stretch out a bit more, laterally, across your designated seat. Occasionally it can be awkward, when a seatmate has not put the armrest down yet, and you have to be the one to do it, sometimes with a little friction against their elbow or thigh.

Armrests are borders, but unclear ones. Standard armrests in the economy section of most airliners are not nearly wide enough for two arms to rest on them. It is often a question of who places their forearm there first; and if you take your arm off—say, to adjust the air blower above your head—the space is fair game for your seatmate. Even in first class, armrests can be vague divisions. An especially gregarious or inebriated seatmate can spill over into your space, acoustically and aromatically, if not exactly physically. An aisle armrest—ostensibly a safe space, whether in first or economy class—is fraught for its own reasons: for instance, if your elbow is hanging off a centimeter too much when a flight attendant pushes the drink trolley past your row, or if you doze off leaning a bit too far into the aisle, where passengers might jostle you on their way to the lavatory.

A lot of hay was made about Jessica Leeds's claim, a month or so before the election, that her armrest "disappeared" when Donald Trump allegedly reached across the seat divide and groped her beneath her skirt on a flight in the early 1980s. Various sites went to some lengths to show that first class seats could not—or maybe *could*—have had retractable armrests at the time that Leeds cites. Some planes around that time most certainly did *not* have such first class seating: first class armrests on these aircraft could not be lifted to allow for heavy petting, and were substantial enough to make even leaning across cumbersome at best. Other contemporaneous airliners clearly *did* allow for such seating configurations, possibly anticipating—if not outright encouraging—in-flight romance.

Motivations for such sleuthing may have seemed tactical enough at the time: Was the claim of sexual aggression true? Were there material facts that might complicate the claim? I will admit that I wondered, too, when I first heard Leeds describe the situation, how the armrest between their seats could have simply vanished. Newer first class seating almost always involves a fixed armrest.

Still, this quibble misses the point. No matter the model of plane, the layout of seats and the maneuverability of the dividers wherein, as we all know, armrests can most definitely disappear. For this, importantly, is the word that Leeds used in her statement: "the armrest disappeared." Whether or not armrests can physically be raised and recessed in between seats, they can indeed seem to dematerialize. They do this all the time.

Louis C. K. once riffed on this potentiality in an episode of *Louie*, where a much larger man inhabits the seat next to his. Louie is barely able to move, with the other passenger overflowing his own seat, in exaggerated form. (Interestingly, by the end of Louie's flight the two seatmates seem to have bonded and become friends.) As most frequent travelers have likely experienced—first class, business, or economy, it really doesn't matter—there is always a chance that a neighboring passenger will extend beyond their personal space and make your trip demonstrably *theirs*. In the case of Donald Trump and Jessica Leeds, the disappearing of the armrest seems to have been done in an aggressive and indefensible style.

And this matters, as anyone who has felt dominated by a seatmate should readily admit. If the situation involves sexual advances or any other misconduct, you might leave the plane feeling disgusted if not outright assaulted, shaking off the residues of what Newt Gingrich at the time dismissed on behalf of Leeds as merely "a bad airplane flight."

Only sometimes this really, really matters. Like when there is real abuse. Like when the bad seatmate is then chosen to become the leader of an entire country. Airplane armrests are never a simple matter of neutral ground; they are subtle barometers of power differentials, and therefore we might pay extra special attention to such spaces rather than overlook them as mere minor partitions. They can become sites of passive aggression, intense contestation, and simmering wrath—and they may be especially tense when it comes to gender, which has been a fraught aspect of commercial aviation throughout its history. Airplane armrests are complex objects, not just technically speaking, but over which charged dynamics play out on a daily basis. We may forget about armrests once we land and walk away from our flights. But most of us know the indignity of these slender separators.

Regardless of the aircraft model or seat configuration, armrests can indeed be made to disappear. People have power, and this is not always a good thing, depending on where you're sitting: an armrest can portend an uncomfortable duration to be suffered through. At the same time, armrests might be championed as durable facilitators of our many differences, the architecture of our impressive capacity for sharing seats.

New Planes

Now I've just spilled a drop of coffee on my armrest, and I'm wiping at it furiously. I feel guilty because the plane I'm flying in is a very new Airbus A319. Blue LED lighting bathes the cabin in a soft luminosity. Each row has a pod above it, also lined by a cerulean strip. The flight attendant call button, when accidentally illuminated, makes the pod glow a complimentary mellow orange. The lavatories, also resplendent in ambient lighting, are incredibly small, with every centimeter of space having been maximized.

The overhead bins swing down, capacious buckets that get heavier as passengers load their roller bags inside. This is altogether different than the overheads of the past, with their flimsy doors and dimensions insufficient for larger and larger luggage coming onboard. These new bins hold their cargo, but are clearly painful to close. I watched our flight attendant wrestle and slam them shut before takeoff, and later when I ask him how he likes working in the newly redesigned Airbus cabin, he rolls his eyes and tells me that each bin weighs 300 pounds, 14 on each side—"do the math." Also, he says the rear galley is terrible to work, cramped as it is next to two adjacent lavatories. I've noticed that the flight attendants, when they are restocking their drink and snack trolleys, have to regulate the flow of passengers using the lavatories.

The entertainment systems are by far the best yet—no surprise there, as the envelope of digital media is increasingly seamless. The total merger of smartphones and in-flight entertainment is almost complete. I'm charging my iPhone in a USB port attached to the seat base in front of me, right next to my leg. My seatmate has their phone plugged in as well; we're a couple happy campers. Just a few years ago, who would have believed it? But in spite of these little luxuries, the passengers around me look depressed. Maybe it's just the early morning flight, or the seats that keep getting tighter and harder, with less and less legroom—there's ample research out there to demonstrate this fact.

So the new planes, for all their efficiencies and extensions of self-entertainment, are also new nightmares. We adapt to the miseries and quickly come to expect the conveniences. Meanwhile, the latest inconveniences conspire against us. The snack boxes are expensive when they are even available, and the temperature is either too hot or too cold. New planes, old problems, a self-consuming circle—this is the ouroboros of airportness.

Airplane Reading I

A few passengers around me devour thick novels adorned with provocative titles in bold lettering. While such airplane reading rarely has the appearance or function of being edifying, these books nevertheless hint at the possibilities for reading beyond the college seminar room, beyond the cozy recesses of home. In 1812 the poet Percy Shelley dispersed messages in balloons over the Irish Sea; more recently, there were short stories on Chipotle cups. A *New York Times* article by Alexandra Alter in 2015 explored the latest iteration of literature out of context, a topic that invites us to ponder the nature of flight:

> Last summer at a writers' workshop in Oregon, the novelists Anthony Doerr, Karen Russell and Elissa Schappell were chatting over cocktails when they realized they had all published work in the same magazine. It wasn't one of the usual literary outlets, like *Tin House*, *The Paris Review* or *The New Yorker*. It was *Rhapsody*, an in-flight magazine for United Airlines.

There's an awkward dynamic in this paragraph: between highbrow literary art, on the one hand, and the disposable culture of flight, on the other. An in-flight magazine, with all its connotations of sticky pages, half-done Sudoku puzzles, and gimmicky ads for bizarre products, seems a curious venue for those best-selling literary writers to share. An in-flight magazine is the nadir of nonliterary writing, the epitome of what we might call "airplane reading" in a disdainful tone. The in-flight magazine's gaudy panoply of consumer items and photoshopped images can make one yearn for the relatively simple ingredients of a trash novel: narrative, plot, climax. How, then, does the in-flight magazine come to be a destination for A-list authors? Could there be something redeeming about this, deploying art so as to be therapeutic or uplifting for otherwise miserable passengers? Or is it merely a well-paying venue for authors hawking their stories?

The *Times* article goes on to describe the growing popularity of arrangements between writers and transit companies—from airlines to Amtrak—as driven by the potential for something particularly rare in the digital age: a "captive audience." Indeed, such an alliance was in the news in another form a couple of years earlier, when Southwest Airlines launched an in-flight reading series of sorts, wherein writers would stand up in the aisles and read to their captive audiences. The word "captive"—used in the *Times* and also in an *L.A. Times* article about the Southwest in-flight readings—is intriguing, given certain associations that airlines would probably rather avoid.

The idea of an airline acting as a "literary patron" suggests that it is not simply bored, plodding herds of air travelers who need the cocktail sipping literati, but rather the despairing writers "in this shaky retail climate" who need the financial largesse of airlines. So the dynamic flips around. But then things get weirder. We learn from this article that *Rhapsody* is not your average in-flight magazine, but is in fact a publication reserved—even *guarded*—for first class passengers. In other words, it has a class status attached to it that then reflexively complements the league of writers with whom we began. The *New York Times* (2015) elaborates:

> Mark Krolick, United Airlines' managing director of marketing and product development, said the quality of the writing in *Rhapsody* brings a patina of sophistication to its first-class service, along with other opulent touches like mood lighting, soft music and a branded scent.

It would now seem that the classy aura of literature reflects and bolsters the ambience of the first class cabin. Our authors are not simply hapless benefactors of the "1 percent," but rather have something to offer that is consistent with the "other opulent touches" appreciated by first class fliers. In some ways, it might even be argued that literary writing not only completes the first class cabin, but also *adds* to it: literature "brings a patina of sophistication" to first class service. This reminds me of Jacques Derrida's famous formulation of the "supplement" as that which is both necessary for self-identity and which *adds on* to self-identity—thereby complicating what the "self" would even mean, isolated and intact. Who is the first class passenger, without the abetting agent of literature? (Don't worry, you won't find any continental philosophy in the pages of *Rhapsody*—there is a line in the sand you do not cross when it comes to airplane reading, even in first class.)

Back to our literary writers who seem at once natural and unnatural seatmates in the first class cabin. The *New York Times* (2015) article goes on to explain exactly how *Rhapsody* works:

> In addition to offering travel perks, the magazine pays well and gives writers freedom, within reason, to choose their subject matter and write with style. Certain genres of flight stories are off limits, naturally: no plane crashes or woeful tales of lost luggage or rude flight attendants, and nothing too risqué.

Naturally. I love this line: "no plane crashes or woeful tales of lost luggage or rude flight attendants, and nothing too risqué." No disasters, no lost objects, no skirmishes, no sex—well, there goes most of what we call "literature." In a startling revelation, we see how the concept of nature is in fact defined through literary parameters. Or, the nature of flight becomes a flight from nature.

As if *Rhapsody*'s agenda isn't clear enough, the article goes on to stress this point, quoting the editor-in-chief Jordan Haller: "We're not going to have someone write about joining the mile-high club." Despite these restrictions, Haller claims, "We've managed to come up with a lot of high-minded literary content."

With in-flight magazines like these, who needs a liberal arts education? Aren't the very "restrictions" that Haller alludes to—exploring them, exploding them, turning them inside out— precisely what drive literature, at its best? Can literature exist—

much less thrive—with this counterintuitive topical constraint? Or, in light of the long history of literary constraint, might this create the optimal conditions for a writer to sit down and, well, write something good?

The article really gets interesting here from a pedagogical standpoint, though that's probably not what they were going for: "Guiding writers toward the right idea occasionally requires some gentle prodding." For instance, it tells the story of Karen Russell being invited to contribute a "memorable flight experience," but when she pitched a story of a multi-hour airport delay chaperoning grumpy teenagers, the editor of *Rhapsody* asked her to reconsider: "He pointed out that disaster flights are not what people want to read about when they're in transit, and very diplomatically suggested that maybe people want to read something that casts air travel in a more positive light." Russell ended up submitting "a nostalgia-tinged essay about her first flight on a trip to Disney World when she was 6."

So what we have here is an acclaimed author asked to contribute something for a magazine, then hemmed in by a mandate qua naturalized assumption that people do not want to think about "disaster flights" while on an airplane. However, the author does not leave in a huff of artistic integrity; Disney World soars in to save the day. Everyone is happy. No one writes or reads anything that might make one think critically about the enterprise in question: *the nature of flight*.

The article offers further examples of *Rhapsody* writers and their chosen—or sanctioned—topics:

[Joyce Carol] Oates . . . wrote about her first flight, in a tiny yellow propeller plane piloted by her father. The novelist Joyce Maynard told of the constant disappointment of never seeing her books in airport bookstores and the thrill of finally spotting a fellow plane passenger reading her novel *Labor Day*. Emily St. John Mandel, who was a finalist for the National Book Award in fiction last year, wrote about agonizing over which books to bring on a long flight.

This final author, Emily St. John Mandel, is an offbeat inclusion, particularly given what we have just been thinking about under erasure—stories of "disaster flights." Mandel's unnamed National Book Award finalist was *Station Eleven* (2014), a postapocalyptic novel that hinges on "disaster flights" par excellence: a highly contagious flu virus travels around the world on commercial jets and kills nearly the entire human population within a matter of weeks. One group of survivors makes their home at the Severn City Airport, which also comes to house an inadvertent "Museum of Civilization." It is a brilliant and moving novel, replete with hauntingly familiar scenes of obsolete airport accoutrements.

In other words, running parallel to *Station Eleven*'s primary narrative is an anticipatory requiem for air travel at large. An early section of the novel delineates an "incomplete list" of things that are no more:

No more flight. No more towns glimpsed from the sky through airplane windows, points of glimmering light; no more looking down from thirty thousand feet and imagining the lives lit up by those lights at that moment. No more airplanes, no more requests to put up your tray table in its upright and locked position—but no, this wasn't true, there were still airplanes here and there. They stood dormant on runways and in hangars. They collected snow on their wings. In the cold months, they were ideal for food storage. In summer the ones near orchards were filled with trays of fruit that dehydrated in the heat. Teenagers snuck into them to have sex. Rust blossomed and streaked. (31)

Needless to say, this kind of literature would hardly be appropriate for the pages of *Rhapsody*. And yet readers will find a tamer story by Mandel in *Rhapsody*. But if they like her writing, they may then buy *Station Eleven* in the airport bookstore for their return trip. What then, when they have veered from the tranquil pages of *Rhapsody*, and are suddenly reading about "disaster flights" in a novel? The status of literature vacillates between approved and illicit, between entertaining the traveling liberal subject and agitating the fragile human in flight. Mandel implicates air travel in the end of human civilization as we know it—this should be code red for the editors of *Rhapsody*.

My mind drifts here, as if catching onto an intersecting jet contrail and following it to my home airport, eleven miles west of the city of New Orleans. This airport is a site of disaster and recovery, at turns. The call sign for the Louis Armstrong airport, KMSY or just MSY, refers to an earlier name: the Moisant Stock Yards. The airport was originally named after John Moisant, a legendary daredevil aviator who crashed and died in 1910 on

the agricultural site upon which the airport would later be
built. For a human pursuit that seems prone to superstition and
overabundances of caution, I am struck by how a fatal crash
lurks behind my airport's simple, pragmatic call sign, evoked
countless times each day as aircraft depart and arrive.

As I write this book the New Orleans airport is in the process
of a wholesale reinvention. A glassy new terminal building,
with an $850 million price tag, is currently under construction
across the runways from the existing hodgepodge of concourses
and gates. The new airport is being billed as a "world class
terminal"—a veritable Xanadu, with the most decadent, if also
minimalist, fixings, so tourists and locals alike may enjoy the
perks, efficiencies, and capital flows facilitated by modern air
travel.

In a famous essay called "Airports: The True Cities of the 21st
Century," J. G. Ballard reflected on his nearby home airport of
Heathrow. Ballard writes, "I welcome the landscape's transience,
alienation, and discontinuities, and its unashamed response to
the pressures of speed, disposability, and the instant impulse.
Here, under the flight paths, everything is designed for the
next five minutes." In the architectural plans for the new Louis
Armstrong Airport, we see bold attempts to ward off and eschew
Ballard's enthusiastic if also bleak diagnosis of postmodern
space. There will be greenery, there will be open areas for music
and art, together suggesting a vibe of relaxation usually reserved
for zones far beyond the tarmac. On the other hand, we may
detect hints of a disaster to come, particularly given the vexed
state of coastal erosion and rising seas—thinking in terms of "the

next five minutes" comes with a cost. In the background of the striking conceptual mock-ups available on the airport's website, the Mississippi River looms, churning and churning, suggesting other environmental limits and flux.

In the many-windowed architecture of the new terminal, we can hear echoes of one of the characters of *Station Eleven*, the latter-day psychoanalytic business consultant Clark Thompson, who lives on at the Severn City Airport even as its name and purpose have become utterly obsolete: "Clark had never thought so much about airport design, but he was grateful that so much of this particular airport was glass. They lived in daylight and went to bed at sundown" (245). The new airport renderings anticipate postapocalyptic life, even as they seem to project a flush and verdant future of air travel to come. But as *Station Eleven* suggests, the end of petromodernity is nigh, one way or the other; what we do with the remains is up to us.

In a book called *Earth*, Jeffrey Jerome Cohen reminds us that "humans have *always* loved their apocalypses" (32). I think about airplane reading's normative sterility, and also the tame futurism of airport design, and I wonder how we might begin to move toward an alternative relationship to air travel. What would it look like for humans to acknowledge the chapter of air travel as coming to a close—even to welcome this, in favor of some other form of travel, migration, habitation? Whether looking at something as seemingly innocuous as in-flight magazines, or as intricate as large-scale airport planning, we encounter the nature of flight, and it is uncertain to say the least. Airportness involves how we have, for better or worse, naturalized this form of vehiculation—but also how flight is subject to change, subject to active reimagining and revision.

I look around me now at the passengers zoning out, turning the pages of their airplane novels, or pushing madly at touchscreens. The engines roar gently outside, and a plastic snack wrapper crinkles somewhere behind me. The concentration of this space-time is bewildering; it's no wonder we try to tune it out, even as it comes back to haunt us on our screens, in our books, and in our conscious and unconscious minds.

Consider the Lavatory

The perky flight attendant on this early morning flight has been plying us with refills of coffee; my bladder is full. And luckily I'm sitting at the aisle, so I don't have to break the contract of the window seat. A quick glance to the back of the plane assures me that there is no line—it's time to go to the lavatory.

Have you ever found yourself inside the lavatory, inspecting your visage in the hazy mirror, staged in the dim light, wondering how long you've been standing there, how much longer you can get away with it before another passenger or a flight attendant knocks on the door? It's a little pentagon of privacy in the otherwise public oval of the airplane. But you can't stay for long.

From the Middle English *lavatorie* and the Medieval Latin *lavatorium*, both from the Latin *lavare* (to wash)—how do our modern airplane bathrooms cling to this ancient appellation?

There is something almost timeless about this space: once you go in and shut the stiff yet flimsy plastic door, everything else in the airplane vanishes, muffled in some near distance. It is a place full of mystery and suspense.

There's the small sink with faucet of uncertain water pressure—is it going to shoot out with surprising force, or just dribble onto your fingers? There are the myriad signs, minimalist icons implying warnings and instructing things like DO NOT OPEN and DEPOSIT WASTE HERE. Red stripes of caution slash through simple humanoid forms. It is a tight space, over-brimming with communications. In the lavatory when the captain makes an announcement, for once it may sound like the captain is speaking to you alone. Occasionally you'll be in there when the plane starts shaking and a calm icon illuminates with a ding, a placid command: *return to your seat.*

Then there is the small molded toilet with its sketchy seat, the hinged and bouncing metal flap at the bottom of the bowl (sometimes laden with soggy toilet paper or worse), and the vortex of "blue juice" sucking into the void. Do you sit or try to stay propped up, awkwardly hovering over the bowl? How clean is this place, anyway? In fact, airlines are usually pretty good at cleaning lavatories regularly and thoroughly (I know—I used to have this job). As germ-filled and claustrophobic as the lavatory may feel when you are in it, it's also likely that it is one of the cleanest public bathrooms you'll ever use.

Once I entered a lavatory and was surprised to see the tiny sink filled with what at first looked like trash. When I looked closer, it was actually a rather careful arrangement of sanitizing napkins—the sink was inoperable, so a clever flight attendant had placed a bouquet of packaged hand wipes in the sink, and taped a note to the mirror instructing the passengers to use these instead of washing their hands. The lavatory became a place for creative problem-solving. Such initiative, such industry!

Down the aisle, passengers sit and stare at the red cartoon that denotes OCCUPIED. Who is in there, and why are they taking so long? But these two experiences of time are so distinct, inside and outside the lav. Outside, in a cramped seat, time drags on and it can be hard to focus on things. But in the lavatory time stands still, and everything is in focus. It's a small, usually windowless room where everything pops into distinction, and yet where everything becomes unnerving, too. Where exactly are you, here? "Lavatory"—the very name bespeaks some sort of untimely place, some space out of joint. What rhymes with lavatory? A priori.

So why do we retain this unusual word? Does it supply a bit more decorum on that most abject space visited during the already uncomfortable experience of flight? The name makes the place sound more regal than its austere reality. As such, the lavatory may function as a metonymy for the whole experience of commercial flight: it's made to sound better than it really is, once we're in it.

Occasionally aircraft lavatories burst into the news: an aging actor doesn't make it to the lav in time, and pees in the aisle; another actor, a bit younger, slams the lavatory door in a huff and gets kicked off the plane; terrorists may use the privacy of the lav to assemble cruel devices or hint at their presence; an artist repurposes one for a spontaneous exhibit on a trans-Pacific long-haul flight. Most of the time, though, lavatories fade into the background.

But here's the thing about this space: while airlines go to great lengths to sell the experience of flight as individuated, personal, and endlessly customizable—the lavatory is the only truly private place on normal commercial airliners. And yet—here's the rub—it's also the only place that is shared by *everyone* on board. It's a paradoxical place, and one that we don't really want to think about too much.

Taro Gomi's classic potty-training book *Everyone Poops* works by showing young children all the shapes and sizes of various animals' excrement ("an elephant makes a big poop, a mouse makes a tiny poop," and so on). The book culminates in a child's bowel movement, with gentle encouragement to do it on the toilet. But the unavoidable premise of the book is that humans are put on the same plane as camels, raccoons, fish, and worms. We're not so different, when it comes to our business.

Isn't this what is finally so embarrassing about the lavatory? It exposes the grand project of flight as so much animal activity. We are less a suave set of individual travelers, donning antimicrobial fishing shirts and maneuvering sporty roller bags. We're more like a migrating collective, not so unlike a wobbly V of Canada geese cruising overhead—another day, another long journey. The lavatory reminds us that everyone poops, and that we are not so special as our job titles or status as frequent fliers would make us believe.

Snacking

It's hard to believe anyone would like to eat pretzels, cookies, or peanuts at this early hour, but passengers around me are gobbling up these snacks offered by the flight attendant.

Why can't airports have working gardens, so that passengers and workers can have fresh fruit and vegetables for snacks, instead of all the sugary and salty crap that is normally proffered? Sometimes I get very discouraged at airports and on the plane when I see all the incessant, mandatory snacking that occurs throughout the journey. If the snacks were healthier, if they had some tie to the place where you are—especially during connections—wouldn't this be better?

Airports require so much open space and offer such unobstructed sunlight, you'd think on-site gardens would be entirely possible, thereby improving the travel experience. Of course there's the air quality issue, tarmac runoff (deicing fluid, oils, and so on), and the problem of inviting animals and birdlife into the relatively enclosed zone of the airfield. I guess airports are not ideal gardening locations, after all. I guess we'll have to stick with pretzels, for the time being. But seriously, is there a future in such snacking? Or is snacking a remnant of the present past, a place we're having a hard time getting out of, like a bad airport delay? Snacking has become a part of airportness, and for airports to become better, so must our relationships with snacks.

Initial Descent

Behold the flight attendant filing through the cabin, picking up peanut wrappers and plastic cups, and gently admonishing passengers who haven't yet put their seatbacks fully upright. We are on our initial descent, and will be cleared for landing soon. As we emerge through the clouds and bank toward the runway, I see seagulls close by, flying below us, but this reminds me of another aspect of airportness that offers no easy solution.

With the blockbuster movie *Sully* in theaters as I write this, and racking up glowing reviews, bird strikes have been in the news again. Before even delving into this topic, though, let's pause to really think about the utterly odd assumption contained in this accepted phrase: bird strikes. This phrase denotes what happens when an airplane collides with a bird, or a flock of birds, usually on takeoff or landing. So: an airplane, weighing thousands if not tons of thousands of pounds, and usually moving under incredible power at anywhere between 63 and 200 miles per hour, depending on the type, plows into a relatively miniscule bird or birds, most likely flying at an oblique angle to the aircraft's trajectory—and we have the audacity to call this a *bird strike*? Why not a *plane strike*?

I have written about this phenomenon on and off for the past seven years or so, but still I cannot shake it: to borrow and adapt a concept from the environmental philosopher Thom van Dooren, I would call bird strikes a regime of violent reversal, wherein the violence of human technology is reconceived in such a way that the violence appears, at least rhetorically, to be coming from outside, from "nature"—from the birds.

Consider how this "problem" is discussed in a brief CNN article "Preventing another 'Miracle on the Hudson' emergency," which recounts US Airways Flight 1549, otherwise known as the "miracle on the Hudson":

> Shortly after pilot Chesley "Sully" Sullenberger took off from New York's LaGuardia Airport in 2009 with 154 passengers and crew, two eight-pound geese flew into each of the plane's twin engines. Suddenly both engines weren't working and Sullenberger faced a gut-wrenching decision.
>
> He had to choose between trying to reach an airport runway, or attempting a daring water landing. As we now know, Sullenberger aimed for the Hudson River—which investigators eventually said was the only choice he could have made that would have saved the plane.
>
> Hollywood's version of Sullenberger's remarkable story premiers in theaters across America this weekend, offering a disturbing reminder to air travelers: We're not the only creatures in the sky.

Look how the geese in question are described: eerily precisely in terms of their weight—eight pounds—and then, somewhat confusingly, given a sort of nefarious intentionality and motivation: the geese apparently, as if in some sort of coordinated attack, flew into both engines simultaneously. But surely this was not what happened. Rather, the plane flew *into* a flock of migrating birds. The reality was probably swift and terrifying for the birds, if equally sudden and difficult to navigate for the pilots. But the way that this article positions the geese as antagonists is striking. The final, bafflingly dramatic statement only heightens this antagonism: "A disturbing reminder to air travelers: We're not the only creatures in the sky." What a confounding as-if epiphany. Again, here we see a kind of strange reversal, where the primacy of human flight is assumed, as though our species has been in the air much longer than birds (or insects or bats, for that matter). Such a brash declaration does epistemic violence to basic ecological awareness, bundling an anthropocentric mindset into the viral buzz of news.

An article from the *New York Daily News*—"The bird-strike threat looms large: With 'Sully' in theaters, the scary reality is that it could happen again"—similarly raises the persistent issue of bird strikes, citing an uptick in incidents since 2009, while also attesting to certain airports' success at installing "avian radar" devices to detect flocks of migrating birds near flight paths and runways. The article states:

> Today, Schiphol, Europe's fifth busiest airport, is installing avian radar to scan the skies around its runways. Siete Hamminga, head of the Dutch radar manufacturer Robin Radar, which is in use at Schiphol, says his product can distinguish risk—more than 6 miles away—by identifying whether an approaching flock is comprised of small, medium or large birds.

Note how "risk" is assessed not in terms of avoidance with all avian flight ways, but rather determined based on the size of birds, and sounding almost like a McDonald's menu: "small medium, or large." And if the birds are small enough, no matter, churn right through the little feathered foes.

Concerning Canada geese in particular, news articles regularly employ the terms "culling," "mitigation," and "Wildlife Hazard Management" when discussing this "avian risk" to commercial air travel. I cannot help but be troubled by this discourse of aggression, and to think how it holds avian flight ways responsible for human danger, and thereby forming a regime of violent reversal. When I consider the rhetoric of bird strikes alongside the admittedly awkward and uncanny use of ultralight aircraft and elaborate puppetry to facilitate whooping crane migration, as van Dooren discusses in the fourth chapter of *Flight Ways*, I find myself respecting the deliberately slow, caring use of technological aeronautics in this latter case study, over the human exceptionalism that fuels commercial flight ways and breeds paranoia around the phenomenon of bird strikes. But I recognize that these separate phenomena, too, are intricately entangled.

Bird strikes are an unpleasant subject to ponder while in flight, much less as we descend and the flocks of seagulls seem to be getting denser, and closer. Still, I don't think we've thought carefully enough about bird strikes, or, more broadly, about our other airborne companion species. When contemplating airportness, birds will always fly into the picture.

Connection

Here we are on the ground again, back in an airport. We deplane much as we enplaned: a herd-like movement shuffling out the plane instead of in. Our visages show signs of relief, and we clench the straps of our bags as we haul them down from the overhead bins. Reassurance, familiar things. Some of us are home, some of us have reached our destination; many more of us are merely connecting, onward to other far-flung places. I am only a quarter of the way to my destination, in terms of geographic space. What is this unsettling space-time, often referred to as a "layover" but more accurately a "connection," a link to another flight, somewhere and nowhere at once?

Up the jet bridge and out the gate, into the mad flow of the concourse. It could be any concourse: it is the universal language of terminal life. The airport is an assault on the senses. A dozen diverse songs blare out from speakers hidden here and there in pop-up shops, kiosks, and alcoves. Bass thumps, voices whine. And passengers flood by, either barking into their phones or staring into palms, thumbing aggressively. Scents of fried food swirl in pungent zephyrs at every food court corner, ethnic notes trying to blend, to bespeak a cosmopolitan panoply, but really they all end up smothered in and reeking of the same frying oil.

Here's what is so bewildering to me: flight is this amazing feat. Watch a dragonfly square circles for a few minutes, or seagulls perform graceful water landings and takeoffs amid cresting waves, and it makes our airliners seem like the most inelegant beasts. And yet, even human flight is incredible. Seeing Airbus and Boeing planes lift into the sky and arc off toward their destinations is a sight to behold, every single time. But this sight has become so banal as to lose its power to captivate, even as it literally uplifts us. With smartphones now saturating airports, you don't even see the wistful faces of lovers having just flown from their mates, or first-time fliers. No, now the small screens in our hands absorb all those romantic feelings, and if passengers look up at all, they appear tired, worn out, sick of the whole thing yet resigned to it.

At the airport, on the long march toward our next gate, I cannot help but feel the tremendous collective letdown that flight has become. This particular airport is undergoing renovations throughout and it seems that every other shop is closed up and plastered over. Moving walkways are out of order, as is the tram that usually takes passengers from the end of the longest concourse to the terminal.

The gates these days have been colonized by fields of stool-height seating zones and recessed booths, with flashing iPads at each seat for ordering food and social media expression. The place is a mess. I pause and consider setting my bag down and ordering a drink, to collect myself, but I notice slimy sautéed onions strewn over the seat and table. Disgusted, I head toward the bathroom to pee.

The bathroom is a traffic jam disaster, with its doorway too narrow to allow graceful passage of people entering and leaving. The hand-soap dribbles out, and the paper towel dispenser is on its last legs. Everywhere, there are outmoded technologies, obsolete signs, and objects in disrepair.

And everyone numbly marches on, onward to flights departing or out to the curbside. The ambience of the airport is one of submission, of dull acceptance. Still the Airport CNN channel regales us with breaking news; still the overpriced food beckons to us, promising this time to taste . . . real.

Figure 6 *Airport underground, photograph by the author.*

I end up downstairs, in a creepy tunnel that is supposed to take me to my gate. There's no one else around. The only signs are some layered EXIT signs that seem to lead further into the fluorescently illumined darkness. I'm somehow suddenly alone in this vast space, this space where I know that thousands of others are trudging, too, nearby . . . but somehow I've entered a bizarre wormhole where no other travelers seem to exist (see Figure 6).

Airportness is the awfulness of these spaces, a quality so dissonant with the actual technics and spectacle of flight just beyond the panoramic windows. I have arrived at this conclusion with some sadness, having worked at an airport, studied airports in cultural texts, and reinhabited them again and again with an open mind, with a sense of wonder and even, at times, exuberance. But this airport is suffocating me with its tackiness; it is a miserable place—you can see it on everybody's faces. And this airport, in its ad hoc appearance and ongoingness, exposes a truth: that as much as airports strive to be modern, embracing the latest communications technologies, the trendiest music, the hippest stuff, they will always be behind the curve, too massive to be nimble, too attached to the clunky technics of flight to showcase or revel in other aspects of human ingenuity.

Play

Stopping by a newsstand to purchase a bottle of water for my next flight, I see toy airplanes for sale. They are miniature airliners, and they light up and make takeoff sounds when you push a button. They are obviously of shoddy quality, not made

Figure 7 *Playmobil "City Action" airport set.*

for heavy play. Such dainty planes seem an odd commentary, as if suggesting the fragility and cheapness of the airliners rumbling nearby.

Toys that represent airport life fascinate me. Take, for instance, the Playmobil "City Action" airport set (see Figure 7).

Here we see many operations of the air journey condensed into a relatively simple, sixty-piece play set. A vehicle does double duty as an air-stair and a scissor-loader with cargo container. The airline worker looks around responsibly as he maneuvers the vehicle on the tarmac. A family looks ready for the trip, toting a duffel bag and dutifully carrying the kid's teddy bear. A plane arcs up into the sky, in the distance. Playmobil presents a quaint, humdrum picture of airportness. That is, until we look a little more closely.

That roller bag, first of all: it's about to get clipped by the scissors-loader, and possibly squashed! Where is the plane, anyway? Should the family be wandering around like that, on the taxiway? Finally, who is that weirdo in the background, with the striped shirt?!? There is nothing to guide us on these murky lines of questioning, but my theory is that these off details have to do with the nature of flight, how every zone and action of air travel relies on an incredible field of *play*, where all protocols and safety measures are punctured by chance and indeterminacy. You never know when you're going to find yourself lost or confused at the airport. You never know when another passenger is going to wander off-script, like the guy in the striped shirt. Airports are full of play, which make them exciting toys and suspenseful realities all at once.

Sparrows

Finally at my gate, sitting here staring out over the bustling concourse, I notice sparrows taking short flights across the beams that line the ceiling. Birds like these live in many terminal buildings. Have you ever seen such out-of-context birds hopping around departure gates, picking at errant McDonald's fries or sipping from sculptural water features? Perhaps not: they fly under the radar, so to speak, minor flight paths amid bigger and louder projectiles. These small birds are neither bald eagles nor rogue Canada geese—they do not demand our attention.

The sparrows do not pose a threat to the nearby planes, although, as one article about sparrows in Detroit's McNamara Terminal reports ("Is Detroit Metro Airport going to the birds?"), bird droppings can become "an issue." The same article describes how when attempts to "shoo" the birds from the space failed, recordings of birds of prey were played throughout the terminal to dissuade the sparrows from getting too comfortable. Still, the end of this article articulates a tenuous acceptance with regard to these flight ways:

> Officials say that if continued attempts fail to force the birds out, they may just accept them as part of the terminal's scenery. And despite the feathered friends, the airport remains a popular choice for travelers.

The final sentence is awkward, as its reference to "feathered friends" is framed by the opening word "despite." Furthermore, the idea of the airport as itself having "scenery" somewhat implodes the internal logic of human air travel: to go elsewhere, across a geographic expanse, to view *significant* scenery. With airports as wilderness spaces, who needs the national park to come? One discovers a fascinating ambivalence here, in the recognition of this dull edge of ongoing survival, or something like it.

A jaunty article from the website *Garden Rant* strikes a similar note, as it waxes poetic about sparrows in the Denver airport:

> So there you are in Denver, stuck in the United terminal while you wait for your long-delayed flight to take off. You're in standard airport mode: phone plugged into a charger, feet propped up on a suitcase, book in hand. You haven't been outdoors since 4 a.m. Eastern time. You live in a tightly sealed world of plastic chairs and gray carpet, and you're starting to wonder if you'll ever get out.
>
> Then something flutters down from the ceiling and lands under the Departures board. You look up, wondering if you imagined it, and then three more things flutter down after it. There are birds in the airport.

The article goes on to celebrate the sparrows for elevating the moods of waiting travelers, and wondering about but not inquiring into the "the airport's official position on the avian population." The writer ponders, albeit pithily, the multispecies entanglement occurring in the airport, noting:

> The birds make their living picking up after people like me. A few crumbs, a couple grains of rice. They must get water somewhere. Maybe they've even built a nest from discarded boarding passes and bits of string from luggage tags.

The sparrows' flight ways in airports are an opening to an acknowledgment of "becoming-together" quite unlike the proximate discourse of "bird strikes." At the airport we witness multiple flight ways in tension, at turns discordant and in quiet harmony.

Craig Arnold's 2009 poem "Bird-Understander" reflects on this particular flight way, while arriving at another feeling, far from the punchy online reportage of sparrows in airports. Here are a few lines from Arnold's poem:

> there is a bird
> trapped in the terminal   all the people
> ignoring it   because they do not know
> what to do with it   except to leave it alone
> until it scares itself to death
>
> it makes you terribly terribly sad
>
> You wish you could take the bird outside
> and set it free or   (failing that)
> call a bird-understander
> to come help the bird

The poet tarries on a dull edge of survival with the bird, seeing not a piece of scenery or a palliative agent, but rather a solitary member of a species in need of assistance. This reminds me of Thom van Dooren's wonderful book *Flight Ways*, which considers the blurry edges of extinction inhabited by five specific bird species. My airport sparrows are not in such dire straits; they are surviving. However, Arnold's notion of a "bird-understander" seems akin to van Dooren's project in speculating about an as-of-yet unacknowledged position that humans might take, accepting and welcoming our multispecies entanglement: "flight ways" as an ontological puzzle that we are part of, and for which we may be in some ways responsible. A puzzle, though, if not to be solved exactly or easily, then at least to be worked with, with deep care and attentiveness—to reprise Arnold's vague yet open phrasing, we are called "to come help the bird[s]." This, while simultaneously understanding that the edge of extinction is all around, and encroaching—if also *usefully* blurry.

The airport sparrows throw off the human exceptionalism of this place, the bustling concourse. They show this tightly secured, rigorously controlled zone to be a curious sanctuary, teeming with life. Keep in mind the many species that inhabit the corridors, caverns, and open fields of airports—these spaces are not solely ours.

Twitter

Below the flights of sparrows, there is an even tinier blue bird summoning me on my smartphone screen: it's Twitter. Here is something I like to do at airports, a way to pass the time and tap into the boundless creativity that otherwise can seem squelched and stifled, if not outright impossible in the suffocating space-time of an airport connection.

When I'm in the airport, I tweet constantly. Sometimes just random observations, but sometimes I make a game out of it:

I like to look up old romantic poems, and juxtapose their lines with serendipitous photographs that I snap on my iPhone. I tweet these image-text collisions and they congeal into a piece of found art as fleeting as the connection itself, but also a record of this otherwise forgotten time. The results are often unexpected and comical, and sometimes poignant—there is something about the mashup of British romanticism and the drudgery of modern American airport life.

I dare you to try this next time you pass through an airport: pull up a Charlotte Smith or William Blake poem on your phone—and then try to pair suitable lines with things you see around the bustling gates. You will notice details you've never seen before; new dimensions of airportness will emerge before your eyes, and before your amused (if potentially confused) audience on Twitter. You may be swayed in unanticipated ways by the poetry of airports. And this may affect how you think about airports—I hope for the better, for all their beauty and imperfections, for all their comedy and errors. In order to contentiously change them, in one way or another, we have to learn to see airports, first.

Breakfast

At a breakfast place I order an herb-and-garlic omelet, but the waitress returns to my table despondent, explaining that they are out of oregano and so they cannot make the omelet with herbs. I point at a jar of oregano above the bar, alongside a dozen other herbs and spices—but it is apparently only decorative. They're not allowed to open those jars.

Why do we tolerate so much simulacra at airports? Why do we accept these spaces as, somehow, *artificial* places? How can we make airports better, as long as we are determined to decorate them with endless fakery?

The simple eggs and toast that arrive could not be more tasteless. Airportness exudes from the food here; you taste it in each bite.

747

Let's head to our gate, for the next flight.

Wait—stop, look at this: a Boeing 747 preparing to board. No matter how many times I've seen these planes, they still take my breath away. Their sheer size and their unusual humpbacks. I've only been on one once, for a short trip from San Francisco to Denver, seated way in the back—it was when I worked for Sky West Airlines, and I was flying non-revenue, standby. I was one of the last ones to board, so I hurried to my seat. Still, I remember the experience vividly: the wide body, and the winglet so far away out my window. The seemingly impossible takeoff speed. Once in flight I tarried by the galley and chatted with the flight attendants, and I wandered the dual aisles, fingers brushing the overhead bins.

Now whenever I see a 747, whether taxiing or parked at the gate, I am simultaneously in awe and confounded by its

Figure 8 *747 cargo liner, LAX,* © *Christopher Schaberg.*

presence, its very aura—all that it stands for and all that it takes
to maintain this way of travel. The 747 represents the apex of
modern commercial air travel in the twentieth century, so many
of the compromises and negotiations between maximizing
capacity while also ensuring comfort and the aura of luxury
for all aboard. If you had to choose a single plane to sum up
airportness, it would likely be the 747 (see Figure 8). But the
plane model is nearly fifty years old, now—and most American
airlines have been cautious to embrace the newer Airbus A380,
which dwarfs the 747. Whenever I see a 747, I wonder: where
are we going, from here? Obviously we cannot go back in time.

I remember when I saw the terrifying dash-cam video of the
747 cargo liner National Airlines Flight 102 that crashed shortly
after taking off from Bagram, Afghanistan, in April 2013. The
plane was transporting military vehicles, and apparently they

became untethered as the plane ascended, and slid back in the plane damaging the flight controls. On the dash-cam video, the plane appears to lose its angle of incline, tilts unnaturally upward, and then falls apocalyptically to the ground, exploding on impact. It was as if the entire century of flight was burning up, everything collapsed into that one aircraft.

I wonder how the new American president is adjusting to his new special 747, Air Force One? What is his favorite feature aboard the presidential jet? Is it the Platonic form of all commercial airliners, or just the necessary superstructure that upholds all other dingy planes?

Colin Farrell

Back on the plane now, an uneventful connection, smooth and for the most part unremarkable. Everything appears to be on schedule. But as soon as we are seated and settled in, word travels through the cabin in hushed tones: Colin Farrell is on our flight.

Passengers around us crane their necks, looking over their headrests, as surreptitiously as possible, to catch a glimpse of the dashing actor. Apparently he is in a window seat somewhere back by the exit row.

By the time the rumor makes its way to our row, we are already pushing back from the gate. Held captive by our seatbelts, we cannot confirm this celebrity sighting, though it seems credible enough: it happens from time to time, an actor or sports star on a regular flight. It always seems hard to believe that the elite would end up on a grimy commercial airliner, in coach class no less. But the complexities of air travel logistics are very real, and sometimes there is simply no faster way to get somewhere; and if first class is full, it's full. Private planes seem readily available, to the rich and famous, but they too rely on elaborate schedules, pilot availability, mechanical check-ups, and so on. Maybe Colin Farrell had to go to a film location spur of the moment, or maybe a personal matter is the cause of his ending up on our flight. Whatever it is, my mind races at his presence on our plane, and I think how lucky we are—even as I am aware of the silliness of such a sentiment. It will, most likely, be a flight as uninteresting as any other. And yet: Colin Farrell is on the plane with us!

Once at cruising altitude, I gradually work up the nerve to visit the lavatory, even though this effectively breaks my sacred contract as the window seat occupant—I am hoping against hope to steal a sidelong glance of the actor on my way past his row. Stray scenes from the film *Miami Vice* flash through my mind. In those brief seconds as I shuffle down the aisle toward his row, I try to psychically connect with Colin Farrell, imagining that he might look my way, smile and nod, or maybe even roll his eyes as we knowingly share a smirk about the inanity of commercial flight. . . . But when I pass his row, all I see is a dark head of hair, close-cropped, attached to an imperceptible face staring out the window, a sky blue polo shirt collar lining the base of a neatly trimmed neckline. The shape of his slumped back *does* seem vaguely familiar, though. It recalls *In Bruges*, the hunch of Ferrell's brooding, ill-fated hit man.

On my way back through the cabin, after using the lavatory, I am startled to see that his seat is empty. Miraculously, Colin Farrell has apparently gone to use the lavatory at the *exact same time as me*; we were mere feet from one another, engaged in our private rituals, so close, and yet so unknowable. And he is still in there! I turn back to see if the door will open, granting me a full body view, but I am swept forward to my seat by a tide of galley trolleys laden with Coke products and miniature pretzels, and the lavatory door remains closed, red figurines crossly illuminated above.

Once I sit back down, the flight settles into a familiar, monotonous rhythm. I forget about Colin Farrell. The palpable buzz in the cabin decreases to a murmur, and then is absorbed altogether by the dull roar of the engines. Passengers lose themselves in seatback screens, iPads, and uncomfortable slumbers. I work on a reader report for a publisher, and revise an essay I have been working on. I zone out, staring into the same blooming clouds that Colin Farrell is possibly also contemplating at that very moment. Around me, people flip through channels on devices attached to the seatbacks in front of them, other gleaming actors grinning, grappling, or gunning each other down, depending on the screen. Occasionally, I think I see Colin Farrell flitting across a screen. Eventually, I too succumb to the flicker of the screens, and I tap on the one staring blankly at me from a few inches away.

In-flight Entertainment I: *Somewhere*

Somewhat reluctantly, I scroll through my entertainment options. The first thing that catches my attention is the 2010 film

Figure 9 Somewhere *in two airports,* © *2010 Focus Features, directed by Sofia Coppola.*

Somewhere, directed by Sofia Coppola. Pay attention and there are lessons about airportness within this movie that would seem to have very little to do with flight, on first review.

Consider how the culture of flight is evoked in the film, in a brief sequence of scenes (see Figure 9). At one point, the main character Johnny Marco (Stephen Dorf) has to fly to Milan for a publicity junket of sorts. We get two very brief airport scenes: one as Johnny and his daughter Cleo (Elle Fanning) enter LAX, and another as Johnny and Cleo exit Malpensa airport. The flight, on the other hand, is completely elided: they arrive at LAX, a single second elapses, and they are in Milan, trudging through the baggage claim.

These momentary scenes would not stand out so much if they were not placed in the *exact middle* of the film. As it is, Coppola has set an international air travel spree at the precise center point of this narrative: the whole artwork balances on this almost instantaneous vehiculation across vast space and considerable time. It is a journey evoked and yet entirely undermined by two brief passages through the gritty endpoints we recognize as cavernous and bland terminalscapes: one for DEPARTURES, and the other for ARRIVALS. Everything else is left out. But we know everything that has happened in between. We can *feel* it, if we've ever traveled across the ocean on a jetliner.

By this move Coppola shows us just what she means by the phrase "postmodern globalism"—a phrase explicitly mentioned at one point in the film, and received with a look of exasperated bewilderment by Johnny.

Postmodern globalism: it might at first sound like an ironic bit of academic jargon dropped into the film to demonstrate just how cut-off from thought Johnny Marco is. But there's actually something to take from this little utterance, and a literary lineage to trace.

Globalism isn't new, of course, and it might not even be "modern." For the sake of this inquiry, though, let's track one way that globalism can be seen to shift from the modern to the postmodern. Ernest Hemingway's modernist novel *The Sun Also Rises* famously explored the malaise of American expatriates in Paris and Spain in the mid-1920s. The main character of that novel, Jake Barnes, is wounded from an airplane accident: he was a military pilot who flew "on a joke front" (15) of the war. For Hemingway, modern globalism involves humans who are instructed to fly planes in the service of conflicts of dubious origins and ends.

Thirty years later, James Baldwin's novel *Giovanni's Room* chronicled another tale of wandering Americans in search of lost identity, again in Paris and Spain. At one point in the novel the character Hella announces that she took a commercial flight in Spain and would never do it again: she claims the plane shook like a Model-T, and it probably *was* a Model-T at one point before it became an airplane (120). Baldwin's globalism in this scene marks another stage on the way to the postmodern: the materials of history (here, a Ford automobile) have been transported, updated, and recycled into another means of travel—but these materials are still haunted by latent limitations and deficiencies. The lampooned passenger aircraft in *Giovanni's Room* functions as an uncertain means of flight— not as existentially dangerous as Hemingway's fighter plane, yet perhaps more disorienting for how it seems to scramble senses of time, space, and belonging (an old car and a newer airplane; Detroit and Spain; being a tourist and trying to escape an initial point of tourism).

Now consider again the airports in *Somewhere*. We could have easily had scenes of Johnny and Cleo in a first class sleeper cabin on a Boeing 777—such scenes would have fit right into the hotel psychogeography explored by the rest of the film. But by placing the flight in a cinematic lacuna, *by only showing us the airport passages*, Coppola effectively exposes the postmodern globalism at work in the film: this is a world where high-speed air travel is no longer a matter of consciousness—it's not even experienced. It's completely taken for granted.

If Hemingway was showing us how people repressed early airborne-inflicted trauma, and Baldwin showed us how the increasing banality of flight meshes with increasingly global (non)identity, Coppola shows us a new phase: flight driven down into the unconscious. In the land of *Somewhere*, air travel is everywhere and nowhere at once. Air travel is the absent presence in the film, and placed as it is at the exact center point of this story, it may very well be the key to the mystery of global postmodernism. A key, however, that the more we turn, the more it seems to throw itself away.

The *New Yorker* critic Richard Brody praised *Somewhere* for how "internalized" the film is. As Brody puts it, "At the same time as the shots show a reality accessible to all, they seem wrenched from the psyches of the characters" ("A Place for 'Somewhere'" 2010). Brody goes on to describe his experience of the film as "feeling as if I had just been cruising around in a high-powered vehicle for an hour and a half, experiencing a strangely original ride through familiar grounds, a peculiar and delightful blend of the grippingly concrete and the dreamily abstracted." He is most obviously alluding to the black Ferrari that Johnny Marco drives around throughout the film; but I wonder if, on another level, Brody's "high-powered vehicle" is also the thundering jetliner above that contemporary life has come to internalize so well. The nature of flight is how it has become an ambient fact, little more than a trace in the sky, a faint thunder on the horizon, always somewhere else.

As much as I like *Somewhere*, though, I can't concentrate on it here. My mind is scattered, as if being in the plane watching this meditation on flight is too much for my brain, my heart. "Somewhere" is an especially daunting word, when you're in flight.

In-flight Entertainment II:
The Force Awakens

I'm lured into another movie by seeing laser blasts shoot across a screen in the row in front of me: it's the new Star Wars installment,

The Force Awakens. Watching *The Force Awakens* again, I am
struck by a minor detail that recurs throughout the film: the
awkward aeronautics of the prized starship the Millennium
Falcon, and its counterintuitive affinities with the ground.

When we are first (re)introduced to the iconic circle-with-
spurs ship, it is referred to as "the garbage," and can be seen with
drab tarps hanging off the gnarly (if stirringly familiar, to some)
fuselage. It is only after a more desirable ship is blown up that the
characters veer off and board the dilapidated Falcon.

When Rey (Daisy Ryder), the heroine of this new movie,
blurts out that she is a pilot and can fly the Falcon, it is a relief
for her newfound comrade qua ex-stormtrooper Finn (John
Boyega), as well as for audiences who are gripped in their seats
as Tie Fighters strafe and decimate the desert encampment all
around them. As the Falcon lifts off at Rey's control, memorable
quadrilaterals of blue flame emitting from the rear, the ship
rises, dips, and scrapes the sandy ground calamitously . . . before
lurching up into the air again, if haltingly. In these suspenseful
seconds it is uncertain whether the Falcon is going to fly, or
crash. During these moments, the friction between craft and
land is shown in illustrious digital detail—only to be disrupted
by the Falcon's impossible ascent into air, graceful as ever.

Later in the film, when Han Solo (Harrison Ford) shows
up to take command of the Falcon, we feel at ease, at last. By
coincidence, Harrison Ford is actually an established pilot—a
pilot who has performed noble mountain rescues, and has
crashed a helicopter (and survived). Possibly some of us know
this as we see him take the helm of the Falcon; others may simply

recall his expert piloting skills in the dicey asteroid belt midway through "The Empire Strikes Back."

Nevertheless, all his prior experience does not keep Han from similarly banging up the Falcon in *The Force Awakens*. During the final act of the film, we see Han and Chewie boldly embark on an all-or-nothing mission to land on the new and improved quasi-Death Star, the Starkiller Base—only to watch the Falcon come out of hyper-drive crashing into an alpine forest and barreling through a pristine snowfield, stopping only as its hull skids up to the edge and nearly off a precipitous cliff face.

This is cutting-edge science fiction colliding into good old-fashioned American naturalism (see Figure 10). And yet still, the Millennium Falcon is able to fly again, undamaged, as the Starkiller Base explodes and the good guys escape into deep space, all worrisome friction left behind.

What is with these disjunctive scenes, wherein the ever-elusive Millennium Falcon impossibly abrades and crashes into

Figure 10 *The Millennium Falcon crashes through trees in* The Force Awakens, *© 2015 Disney, directed by J. J. Abrams.*

various planetary surfaces, only to reemerge airborne and intact? How exactly is the spectacle of this perilous friction playing to a common (if unspeakable) desire?

These scenes are terrifying and thrilling moments in the film, perhaps in part because they may call to mind (unconsciously, even) recent commercial airliner debacles caught on smartphone video and shared online. To take just one example, consider the case of Asiana Airlines Flight 214, July 6, 2013, when a Boeing 777 touched down too soon at the San Francisco airport, grazing the seawall before flipping on the runway, breaking off its tail and bursting into flames. The "mishandled landing" ended up killing three people and injuring many others who barely escaped the flaming wreckage. Almost immediately, photographs and videos snapped by survivors on the tarmac went viral; similarly, photos and video footage captured by passengers waiting in the nearby terminal showed the scene from a distance. The unifying aesthetic—blasted runway, crumpled airliner—suggests a readiness to document and almost immediately widely share precisely such a spectacle: the high stakes of friction when it comes to air travel.

The Asiana accident and its digital aftermath evince a disturbing fascination with seeing commercial airliners after unintended impact. And as smartphone equipped passengers, we are prepared for this, ready to quickly record the niceties of our failed aircraft. The web is littered with thousands of similar scenes, widebody airliners askew and crumpled. And aren't these the very vessels that lend to the Millennium Falcon its uncanny feeling of familiarity and cramped creature comforts? What is the Millennium Falcon, if not a glorified (if still intimately shabby) Boeing or Airbus? And so why do we relish seeing the Falcon carom of sandy ground, trees, and snow throughout *The Force Awakens*?

We know that air travel is statistically one of the safest ways to travel; but we also know that when it fails, the results are often fatal, and gruesome. The Millennium Falcon's near-crash scenes in *The Force Awakens* satisfy an urge and a desire to see the impossible pulled off: the wingtip chip on takeoff, the botched landing, the sudden plummet, the hard skid across solid ground . . . all the realities that haunt the everyday routines of modern air travel.

We understand that the maintenance of friction upon takeoff or alighting is always a deadly risk—yet we enter into this gamble day in and day out, expecting things to work fine while also so easily mesmerized at the viral spectacles of flight disasters. *The Force Awakens* channels—or feeds into, or both—a new media trend wherein we devour such spectacles. This is the metaphysics of friction, a captivating surreality represented on screens both big and small: it is the failure of flight, and its eager consumption.

Overwhelmed again, I turn off the screen and stare out my window, at snowy mountains below, shadowy canyons and craggy peaks, landscapes not entirely unlike the terrain of the Starkiller Base I had been watching minutes ago.

Airplane Reading II

This is the longer flight today, with hours of time ahead of me still to kill. But *killing time*: isn't that a terrible expression? Time, being the only thing we have, in a certain sense—why would we ever want to annihilate it? Especially when here we are up in the air, soaring through the sky? As long as we think of the time of air travel as time to kill, there will be no easy way to make the spaces therein much better.

These thoughts entertain me for a few minutes, as I watch the landscape below turn into an irregular grid (I'm back in a window seat), but soon enough I'm ready for something else. I can't stop thinking about the first class magazine *Rhapsody*, and I start to wonder how I might procure a copy. This is airplane reading, rarified—and I am curious to know what's really in there, how this publication merges literariness with the privileges of first class air travel.

As I do not fly United Airlines regularly—and when I do, not in first class—I assume I will have to convince a United gate representative to smuggle a copy out of a waiting airliner, and give it to me. I have the scenario all worked out in my head: the light conversation; the no-pressure request; the agent's furtive walk down the jet bridge, and back; the handoff; the score. I imagined the glossy pages sliding illicitly across my fingers as I began to adjust my critical eyes before this flying center of the world. . . .

On a whim I Google the magazine, using the Wi-Fi onboard this plane, and the result shatters my fantasy: there it is, *Rhapsody*, all issues available for download, displayed in tidy grid of thumbnail covers—no first class itinerary required. Well that was anticlimactic.

I download an issue at random, January 2016, with Samuel L. Jackson chilling on the cover wearing gold high-top sneakers, the United logo directly under the sole of Jackson's left foot. What am I in for, here? Am I ready to enter the opulent world of elite airplane reading, even back here in cramped economy class? Is it uncouth that I'm reading this United publication on a Delta jet? Will I be found out? Will it matter? Of course not. Privacy rules the world, up here. (To a point.)

Let's back up a minute, to ask: What is an in-flight magazine? Not *Rhapsody*, but a regular in-flight magazine, like *Hemispheres* or Delta's *Sky*? Some unifying features come to mind: an introductory note from the CEO stressing the airline's safety record, progress, challenges, and opportunities that lie ahead. Full-page ads for springy sneakers guaranteed to eliminate back pain. Articles featuring destination cities and glamour shots of blond, beaming sales representatives beckoning readers to join a dating service based around the mid-day meal, with testimonials evincing true love finally found. Promotions for the airline's loyalty program, promising perks for joining their family. Route maps toward the back, in addition to beverage lists, aircraft models and stats, and simplified airport diagrams for major hubs.

The normal in-flight magazine works throughout to remind me that I am participating in air travel, and encourages me to repeat this activity—to make it more and more a part of my everyday life. If there is something like a Weltanschauung of the in-flight magazine, it may be that in these pages *is* the whole world, poured out glittering, airborne, and replete with everything I need for survival, sustenance, and success. The in-flight magazine wants to make all of human life seem circumscribed by and oriented around air travel. This again is airportness, reissued each month and disseminated into seatback pockets everywhere.

But now I am sitting here looking at the latest issue of *Rhapsody*, and it's nothing like this.

First off, I should be stretched out in a first class seat, up front in a United Airlines jet, sipping complementary whiskey from a real glass tumbler. Instead I am scrunched in this hard, squeaky seat way back in row 19, and I have the magazine open on the screen of my computer that can barely open. The magazine is out of place and unglossy, and I am not its proper reader. A stained paper cup of lukewarm tea rests an inch away, on the tray table's circular-indentation. On my screen a perky animation in the lower right-hand corner of the magazine invites me to virtually flip its pages. I have stumbled into an uncomfortable contradiction here, wherein the thing supposed to be shielded from common use turns out to be accessible to all (at least in theory), in the vulgar form of a downloadable PDF. From this distance, from this contradictory perspective, I want to see what this in-flight magazine says as a whole piece.

I'm following a well-trod path. Roland Barthes's 1957 *Mythologies* was a slim book that collected the author's pithy semiotic analyses of various contemporaneous advertisements, items in the news, and other oddities. It is one of my favorite works of criticism and has served as indirect inspiration for my previous inquiries into the culture of flight. Right now, though, I want to adopt Barthes's style more directly.

In his 1970 preface to the book, Barthes notes that his method emerged at (and worked for) a precise moment in the history of criticism—a time "which belongs to the past" (8). Barthes also underscores the need for ideological criticism to become "more sophisticated" as consumer culture accelerates, as what is "significant" becomes mobilized and normalized in ever new and frightening ways. In the in-flight magazine, and in *Rhapsody* in particular, we see a distillation of signifiers in such a form that everywhere resists and therefore calls out for sustained ideological critique. Class assumptions and power dynamics race across the pages, numbing the reader to the social structure while simultaneously piquing habits of consumption and desire. Given this dense text, I wonder what it might look like to reinvigorate Barthes's shrewd if succinct method, by way of considering the *Rhapsody* issue of January 2016.

The magazine is, perhaps not surprisingly, comprised mostly of advertisements: for high-end apparel, luxury items, and hotels. Occasionally a more plebeian object appears, like a Colavita olive oil ad that awkwardly instructs: "Think Outside the Bottle." I don't really get the point of this twist on thinking "outside the box"—especially within a context that seems desperate to reaffirm the status quo of class differences and income inequity.

For instance, there is a wristwatch advertised that is roughly the amount of my entire home mortgage. (The Graff Mastergraff Ultra Flat Icon Skeleton 43 mm, $211,000.) A brief article about the McLaren 570S sports car states, nonchalantly, "A car with technology like this, for under $200,000, is a steal." That amount, $200,000, keeps coming up as if it is pocket change—perhaps subtly making one's first class fare seem not so expensive, after all. In an exclusive interview, Samuel L. Jackson expounds on his choice to star in the movie *Snakes on a Plane*: "I was like, *Hell yeah*—I want to see this movie, and I want to see *me* in it." Ego and exclusive self-worth are at a premium in the pages of *Rhapsody*.

The maximalist language of luxury accumulates over the course of the ads, and spreads out over an assortment of things and experiences:

> The World's Most Innovative Luggage Has Arrived—T. R. S.
>   Ballistic ("self-balancing")
> "Quite simply, the world's finest fire pit & grill"—Cowboy
>   Cauldron
> A Luxurious Destination—Merrick Manor
> Home Sweet Hotel—LEVEL furnished living
> Artistic Tile ("absolutely worth it")

Hello Opportunity—Artivest ("access exceptional investing")
But then there are more straightforward and palatable pieces, like the one-page feature on the Italian appetizer staple, melon and prosciutto. The basic message is how good food can involve quality ingredients, and fewer of them at that. The final piece in the magazine is a short personal narrative by Mark Vanhoenacker, 747 pilot and author of the 2015 bestseller *Skyfaring*, recalling the time Neil Armstrong was a passenger on one of his flights. Vanhoenacker waxes positive about views from above, linking space rockets and airliners by the aerial visions they afford.

The Vanhoenacker piece is part of a series of features called "Plane Spoken," penned by authors of the moment, each somehow or another relating to flight. This is where the aforementioned A-list authors normally appear. But while the *New York Times* article made it sound like *Rhapsody* featured literary writing *throughout*, it turns out that this "high-minded" content is given a *single page*—namely, the last page of the magazine. Literature then subtends—while also being doomed to follow, to merely conclude—the dominating ad force of the in-flight magazine.

Here's the funny thing about *Rhapsody*, though: there's very little in it at all that lets you know it's an *in-flight* magazine. There's the United logo on the front cover, and there are two "Fly the Friendly Skies" advertisements within the pages, but otherwise—*nothing* about air travel, or the fact that you are (or should be) sitting in a jetliner while you read it. In many ways *Rhapsody* is the obverse of a normal in-flight magazine, subsuming all the aviation iconography and airline branding under the far more aggressive campaign of luxury living. Human air travel is normalized not through excessive denotation, but through a kind of connotative understatement, wherein a certain standard of life is suggested to be naturally contiguous with first class flight. The nature of flight is to accumulate wealth at the expense of others—to soar above the rest.

The "Plane Spoken" column with its theme of flight seems to stand in contrast to most of the magazine—which barely announces its status as airplane reading. This is air travel refined, meditated upon self-reflexively, as if already accepted to be as natural as breathing. And not only flight, but also a set of property relations. Wealth and flight are deemed duly natural in these pages. *Rhapsody* is no mere in-flight magazine, and not just because it contains the works of best-selling authors. It posits the nature of flight and the history of class struggle as coterminous, calmly in balance. *Rhapsody* displays progress as if at cruising altitude, entirely on course.

Still, we seem to know that we're not on course, that something has to change—not just with airports, but with human inhabitance of the planet at large. As confused as Trump's harangues about airports are, we might admit that he's onto something: air travel *has* become more tense and stressful of late; it doesn't *feel* like progress any more (if it ever really did). To make this experience better, though, means not just improving airports. We have to address class disparities. We can't continue on with people divided by net worth, and rewarded accordingly. This is no way to move forward.

Plane Sighting

A glint of light catches my eye out the window. It's there and gone in a flash.

One of the weirdest, most fleeting window seat views is when you look out and see another plane, flying past you in the opposite direction, and it looks near enough that for sure you are going to collide with it. Of course you don't; it whizzes by unnaturally quickly, perceptual speed doubled by your own vector, engine vapor spewing behind . . . and you never see it again.

It's an uncanny twin flight—one hundred or so people headed somewhere else, away from where you are headed. This is what

I saw a few moments ago, another plane shoot past my window, too fast to see the livery or even the tail, maybe red, startlingly right there and then gone. What was this plane? How could I ever know? Well, given a clear connection on my phone, I could try to use Siri to "see which plane is flying overhead." This app is meant for use on the ground—not on the plane. I suppose I could use a flight tracker app, which toggles me, the observer, higher up to a satellite view of planes beneath. But this lateral view of planes out the window? It's uncanny.

I think a lot about the common experience of noticing airliners in the sky, from down below. It's an obsession of sorts. But I am less interested in identifying the specific planes and their mapped lines of flight. Rather, I find myself wondering about the feelings and sensations that such sightings produce, if only for an instant. J. G. Ballard's novel *Super-Cannes* begins as a catalog of such sightings, with incidental publicity planes puttering by every few pages: "droning engines of light aircraft trailing their pennants across the cloudless sky, news from the sun of furniture sales, swimming pool discounts and the opening of a new aqua-park" (37). These planes do not factor into the main plot of the novel, but nevertheless punctuate the story with their routine, hovering presence.

Artist Hiraki Sawa's ten-minute video *Dwelling* (2002) considers a similar phenomenon, but Sawa locates plane sighting in an unexpected context. *Dwelling* begins outside an ordinary apartment. We approach; we enter and ascend a staircase. At first, upon entering, everything seems stunningly ordinary; it's just a plain apartment. Suddenly we see airplanes on the floor. Or is it a taxiway? From the outset, Sawa plays with familiar perceptions of environment, the interior-exterior divide, spatial logic, and ground. Next, we see a few planes on a small table. Then a still shot of a bed, stark white sheets and cover pulled back. Domestic and transit things commingle, if at unexpected scales.

The scene cuts to a carpeted floor with jetliners parked in front of shelves full of what appear to be LPs. Then, unbelievably, before our eyes, one plane takes off—it moves forward and arcs up, right off the carpet. Another plane takes off from the bed. Back on the small table, multiple aircraft taxi, take off, and land (see Figure 11).

Soon, planes are zooming around the room; they fly in and out of a door barely ajar. These are model airplanes—little toy jets yet realistic in their forms, precise lines of flight, and their shadows on the carpet below. Accompanying the panoply we

Figure 11 *Still from* Dwelling, © *Hiraki Sawa (2002).*

hear audible jet engine roars; shrieks of turbine fans fade in and out as the planes enter and leave the frame. Many planes soar at what appears to be cruising altitude, flying in dizzyingly close proximity to one another through the apartment kitchen. A plane lands on the counter and taxies to a stop. An espresso machine nearby eerily resembles an air traffic control tower. Three planes fly past a washing machine. Planes line up on final approach before landing; they barely miss one another and fly directly over me, or at least over my video-eye vantage point. A quiet cacophony of planes, they pass in the hallways and soar through still domestic space. Is this really even an apartment? On the floor by the bed there appears to be an entire airfield full of planes, lined up and ready for flight.

Outside one of the apartment windows, we see clouds race by in the actual sky. Looking up from the carpeted ground, a light bulb becomes an eccentric cloud and planes trace contrails in the ceiling material.

The final shot of the video shows a full-scale jetliner outside the apartment window in the distance, on its approach to land at an airport somewhere near but beyond the horizon.

What exactly is going on here? Hiraki Sawa has converted an interior living space into a hyper-reality replete with off-scale yet familiar flying objects. *Dwelling* warps expectations of big and small and collapses operative concepts of inside and outside. But it also seems to ask the viewer to consider what happens to perceived ordinary space when you add airplanes—typically large-scale objects—flying around the confined space of a small apartment.

Once, while walking through the meadow in front of my parents' house in northern Michigan, I saw a small plane out of the corner of my eye, and it looked like it was in a stall, falling vertiginously. Only when I turned to look, it was a Cooper's hawk plummeting after its prey. I was ready for it to be a plane, though—I was primed for a plane sighting. Years later, I remember camping in the so-called wilderness of Arizona, and hearing the muffled thunder of planes far overhead throughout the still desert night. A discontiguous moment? Maybe not. In a certain cosmic sense, to rephrase Wallace Stevens from "Thirteen Ways of Looking at a Blackbird," *a canyon and an Airbus are one*. And rocks are another kind of furniture. In Davis, California, where I lived when I was in graduate school, gray-green C5 Galaxy cargo planes would float over town in what looked like slow motion on their descent toward Travis Air Force Base. These planes had a warping effect on everything on the ground: speed and size were distorted, and a small-town community tarried with airborne militarized force.

These days, I feel ambivalent about the F16s that regularly tear open the sky over my home in New Orleans. They frighten me, yet they also demand a kind of acute (if brief) attention, if not awe. Perhaps these sightings suggest a contemporary shift in that time-worn aesthetic category of the sublime. In *Dwelling*, Hiraki Sawa seems to be getting at a compelling new world experience, a perceptual event that I call "plane sighting."

Plane sighting is not the same as plane "spotting"—for the latter is about strategic observation or trained perception involving naming, categorizing, and collecting. Plane spotting is an activity that generally focuses on the make and model of aircraft, whether on the ground or in the sky. It is a form of recreation, a pastime—even a form of natural history in the lineage of Linnaeus. Plane spotting is concerned with seeing airplanes and fitting them into a neat and tidy epistemological framework: types, trajectories, titles.

Plane *sighting*, on the other hand, is an affective experience—not always pleasant but always, when it happens, unavoidable in terms of what it evokes, even when it's confused or uncertain. As Michelle Tea writes at one point in her book *Black Wave*, "From her windows she could see the planes in their holding patterns above SFO. Bright lights shining in the sky, just sitting there, not moving" (51). We know that the planes *are* moving—that's what a "holding pattern" is—but it's the perceptual experience that counts: they appear eerily still. And like so many plane sightings, this appearance in the novel is a mere passing event, of no consequence.

Plane sighting involves those brief and common glimpses of aircraft in the sky, planes that can quickly pass beyond the horizon of perception or linger there for a few weird seconds (see Figure 12). It's seeing uninteresting planes doing entirely expected things. Plane sighting is fleeting: it eludes control and perceptual grasp. It's that glint of metal in the sky or a vague drone/thunder/roar somewhere off to the west and above. It's almost sublime—*almost*. But contrails fade fast, or waft into ambiguous stripes across the sky. And as Sawa relentlessly insists, plane sighting is oddly quotidian. That is, plane sighting is inextricably linked with our washing machines and coffee pots, our shoes and our bathroom sinks.

Figure 12 *Plane sighting, photograph by the author.*

By saturating an ordinary domestic space with ordinary planes, Hiraki Sawa reminds us that such planes always already saturate our worldview. Yet at the same time, acute or critical plane sighting could, perhaps, remind us to notice our surroundings and to regard scalar distinctions: pretzel wrappers on the floor; someone with a raspy cough a few rows back; a dead insect trapped in the window next to my head; a Delta Airlines 757 on final approach, a mile below. A crushed water bottle in the trash can. Another human next to me, communicating on her smartphone.

It's peculiar that ordinary airplanes in the sky might draw our attention to the profound thingliness of things. But *Dwelling* seems to suggest that plane sighting might have such potential. Residual contrails turning into zigzag puffs. A low commuter plane with blinking lights at dusk. I live on a planet, somewhere between ground and space—and a part of both at once.

Outside my window and a ways off, another plane races off toward someplace else, miniscule against a gathering bank of stratus clouds in the distance.

Higher Still

Back on my entertainment screen, what's this? A commercial that originally aired for the 2016 Super Bowl, now replayed on this flight between movies. It's a video that has been praised as "breathtaking" and "sweet," a synesthetic overload advertising the 205-mph Audi R8 V10 Plus.

The Audi commercial depicts a resigned, aging astronaut deep in the funk of nostalgia: namely, for the golden era of manned spacecraft, moon-bound in all their glory. He seems destined to chronic melancholia, until a younger man—his son, perhaps—decides to jar him out of his stupor, interpellating: "Okay commander; come with me."

Walking out the front door the younger man holds up a car key, offering the latter-day astronaut the driver's seat. Yet this is a purely symbolic gesture of control—the automobile key has of late been castrated, turned into a "keyless entry remote."

The curvaceous gray car shoots away from the home and careens around an ocean-abutted, moonlit highway, and the forlorn astronaut's face at last creases into a restrained grin. As a *GQ* article helpfully explicates, the vehicle is "rekindling his

Figure 13 *Audi and Bowie, two starmen.*

love for sustained acceleration which he picked up from Apollo rocket launches." A montage of spacecraft memories—boarding capsule, firing engines, shaking cockpit—is intercut between the primary scene of the two men, basically night driving.

As David Bowie's 1972 tune "Starman" bursts into its familiar chorus, the screen goes black, and we read these bold words: "Choosing the moon brings out the best in us."

This commercial is worth reconsidering in conjunction with Bowie's final and nearly contemporaneous music video, "Blackstar," which opens with an eerie image of a tattered astronaut reposed in a rocky landscape, whose sun-shielded helmet is opened only to reveal a blackened skull. In the bizarre world of the music video, this starman's journey has ended hauntingly in esoteric ritual and uncanny fetishism.

It's clear that the Audi R8 commercial is tugging on predictable heart chords: aging twentieth-century heroes, parent-child bonding, and the old standby of a really fast car. But what else is going on here? There is the not-so-subtle equation drawn between *aerial velocity* and *road speed*: this equation is a well-worn trope—recall *Top Gun*'s young Tom Cruise racing a fighter jet on takeoff with his motorcycle on the tarmac—but what is interesting about it here is that the rush of acceleration is obliterating not only space forward, but time in reverse, bringing our astronaut *back* to another (better?) time. In regarding the lost age of space exploration, we see the aging starman relegated to the ground. In his gas guzzling coupé, the aged astronaut hurtles into a future that he seems utterly uninterested in.

We may have the $175,000 Audi sports car, but we no longer have the old promises or futuristic fantasies of space travel. The Concorde has long been grounded, the space shuttle program retired. The latest independent space initiatives seem to keep blowing up in the desert. Deep space may still hold mysteries and opportunities for discovery, but they are more likely to be deeply humbling and existentially unsettling. More like Bowie's Blackstar than Audi's Starman (see Figure 13).

Recalling the *Rhapsody* magazine ads from earlier, here is another object that retails for $200,000—an insidious act of juxtaposition given its original Super Bowl context, suggesting that consumers can so easily choose between a $200,000 car and a $2 bottle of Bud Light. Of course, this is the same sleight of hand that Donald Trump's presidential campaign used to gain incredible momentum: suggesting to people that Trump was an everyman, when in fact he had every exceptional advantage that most of his supporters never had, and never will.

Meanwhile, we continue to fly on these besmirched airliners, humble passengers buckled into our seats—we are not quite astronauts, but neither are we innocent stargazers. David Bowie famously did not like to fly on airplanes, and yet he continues to supply us with some of the most standby paeans to space travel. We embody a similar ambivalence, capped at a lower altitude: we still desire the uplift of flight, while yet knowing its banality, and bracing for its ever-increasing indignities. I don't want to watch another commercial on this screen.

Entanglements

I am feeling disenchanted, and a little bored. Craving something tactile, I pluck the safety briefing card from the seatback pocket. I am looking at its familiar illustrations and narrative instructions. One woman, stone-faced, leaps from the plane onto the evacuation slide, clutching a wrapped baby to her

Figure 14 *Safety briefing card detail.*

chest—the simple downward curving arrow belies whatever terrifying scenario has led to this moment (see Figure 14). Airportness is a low-frequency existential hum that wraps the journey from beginning to end.

Figure 15 *jetBlue safety briefing card, circa 2004.*

This scene reminds me of another safety briefing card that existed on jetBlue airplanes from the early 2000s. I scanned it once and still have it somewhere on my computer. I rummage around until I find it. Here it is (see Figure 15).

jetBlue used humor and exaggeration to get its messages across, both in terms of safety and general etiquette. One instructional no-no depicts a plate with a fish on it; the idea is that your seatmate would be grossed out by the smell—*fish stinks*. This is a reminder that on the plane, passengers ought to be sensitive to the environmental constraints of the space: there is only so much air being circulated (and recirculated), and a single fish can make the place reek real fast. jetBlue advocates basic courtesy while traveling.

The jetBlue briefing card was one of the more honest (and playful) examples in this rather bland genre: instead of showing how passengers should brace for crash landings, jetBlue simply advised passengers to "be nice." It is as if the flight was not just about the miles traveled, but also about humanity at large and how we act in the world. Safety briefing becomes something like a crash course in ethics.

I put away my computer and the safety briefing card, and pull out the latest *New Yorker* magazine that I've brought along for the trip. Flipping through the pages, I notice a profusion of full-page airline ads—perhaps it's just that I'm flying, but I can't help observing the relentlessness of these spreads. It's always fascinating to me to see how airlines peddle their brands by hitching them to various philosophies or worldviews. Here is a Lufthansa advertisement that reads:

Hassle-free travel from 16 U.S. gateways.
On-time arrivals in over 100 European cities.
As dependable as a shoulder to lean on.
All for this one moment.

A picture shows two snoozing passengers, a female's head tucked into her male companion's shoulder. It's straightforward enough, but consider the odd treatment of time in the ad: dependable . . . for this *one* moment. Let's be honest: airplane trips rarely feel like a single "moment," and airlines are notoriously unreliable when things go awry. But even if an airline was proven to be fantastically "dependable," wouldn't this mean for more than one single moment? The small print stresses this point, demanding that we "trust one of Europe's most punctual airlines to get you where you want, when you want." Punctuality is inherently linked to time passing, thus eroding again the insistence on "this one moment" floating above. The reassuring language in this advertisement glosses over deep contradictions in the philosophy of the air journey (see Figure 16).

As if this were not enough, the ad concludes with the slogan, "There's no better way to fly." Curiously, right next to this line is Lufthansa's logo, a simple silhouette of what appears to be a goose or some sort of large waterfowl in flight. This cannot help but suggest that there *are* better ways to fly: for instance, if you're a bird. No matter: the ad does its work, suggesting a put-together airline replete with a natural avian icon as its signature. The goose appears twice in this ad, once at the bottom and once

Hassle-free travel from 16 U.S. gateways.
On-time arrivals in over 100 European cities.
As dependable as a shoulder to lean on.

Trust one of Europe's most punctual airlines to get you where you want, when you want. Visit lufthansa-usa.com.

There's no better way to fly.   ⊘ **Lufthansa**

A STAR ALLIANCE MEMBER

Figure 16 © *Lufthansa.*

floating above the woman's shoulder, on the headrest of her seat. The ad seems to sigh, *remember the birds.*

And it's finally this bird image that haunts me—here we are in the thick of airportness, back with the birds. There are so many tensions between humans and birds when it comes to sharing the air—and when these strains pop, things can get unpleasant

Figure 17 *Water evacuations, real and imaginary.*

fast. We've already observed how Sully's disabled Airbus 320 managed to land safely in the Hudson River in January 2009, after its unfortunate run-in with a flock of Canada geese. News coverage of Sully's flight seemed to reaffirm some of the more standard diagrams on emergency briefing cards: the photos of the passengers exiting the plane were all too reminiscent of the instructions for just how to do so (see Figure 17).

Unlike the subtler Lufthansa ad, US Airways Flight 1547 made clear that being entangled with birdlife is not the ideal state for airplanes, not to mention the humans in the airplanes. Or maybe that while certain amounts of entanglement are necessary for life on the planet, the airplane takes it one twist too far.

After the passengers were rescued from the sinking plane, many commented on the frigidness of the Hudson River: it was as if their encounter with the birds had caused them to really experience the elements. It turns out that river water in New York in January is cold! Here, entanglements with nature became too intimate for comfort: the plane flew into a V-formation of migrating birds, and the outside permeated the inside—first as the stench of roasted geese filled the cabin, and then as the climate controlled airliner was inundated with flowing river water and sank to the bottom of the Hudson. When it comes to air travel, our tidy boundaries demarcating inside from outside can quickly collapse: a smelly tuna sandwich can break the allegedly inalienable rule of private space, and geese that go through a turbine fan can be more stinking than—and demand as much storytelling as—a dead albatross.

In the aftermath of Flight 1547, stories of bird strikes flooded the news. The sensational topic was gradually seen to be banal, as a simple Google image search will reflect: search for "bird strike" and you'll immediately be faced with a tidy grid of plane wreckage, blood, and feathers (see Figure 18).

Google image search results present us with many scales and perspectives, and position us on the outside, looking in— prompting us to select an image. We're suddenly a long way from Lufthansa's aspirational goose: the position of the bird fancier here, on the cusp of the Google image matrix, is the same as the

Figure 18 *Google image search, "bird strike."*

position of the modern computer user—and thus also the same as the position of the modern air traveler selecting a seat.

On most airline websites, or on a smartphone app, we can view the seat map for each flight and decide if we like our seats or if we want to upgrade to various levels of betterment, offering extra inches of legroom for nominal fees (see Figure 19). This one moment, indeed.

Like an aircraft seat map, a Google image search allows us to choose our bird strike—and in each case, each episode offers its contact narrative, gory remains, and an unsettling sense of environmental inevitability. Read enough stories of bird strikes, and you gradually realize that there is no empirical way to avoid bird strikes, aside from emptying the sky of birds—a Sisyphean task that we nevertheless may very well have already started to work on. To some, this might not sound like a bad option; to others, it reeks of ecological ignorance and precipitous ecosystem imbalances. If this dilemma sounds at all familiar, it may be because many of us witnessed it once in 3D on the movie screen, taking place on a moon called Pandora. In fact someone

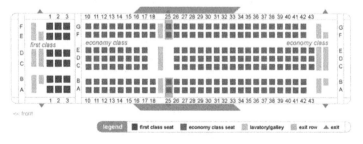

Figure 19 *Aircraft seat map.*

is watching that movie right now on their seatback screen, three rows away from me. I saw it on my way back from the lavatory.

In James Cameron's 2009 blockbuster *Avatar*, an exploitative, proto-American corporation is colonizing the native people (the Navi) who live on the moon Pandora in the year 2145. The Navi are required to relocate, and their sacred tree is violently toppled in order to allow the mining company access to a very valuable resource known as "unobtanium." In a sort of perverse wish image reproduction of the fall of the Twin Towers, the Navi people run in fear as the tree collapses on top of them, fire and smoke swirling around.

In this overdetermined environmental allegory, the Navi pray to their parallel world and are pleasantly rewarded with a form of vicious yet utterly natural retribution aimed at the earthlings: in the penultimate battle of the movie, the heavily military-aided company, fully armed with not-so-futuristic helicopters and aerial bombers, encroaches on one of the sacred, "wild" spaces of the moon. At this point, the Navi are trembling with fear, and unsure whether or not their prayers to the organic network have been heard. All of a sudden, the flying reptiles that we have become familiar with over the course of the film swoop in, autonomously yet as a stirring collective, and they debilitate the armed aircraft by hurling themselves into the turbofans and disrupting the flying surfaces. The empire strikes; birds strike back (see Figure 20).

In other words, *bird strikes* cause the earthlings to quit their mission, and the moon Pandora is restored to its state of natural equilibrium: an enlightened, conscious balance of species who live symbiotically, and in peace. In the end, the remaining

Figure 20 Avatar, *© 2009 20th Century Fox, directed by James Cameron.*

humans are seen humbly boarding their own spacecraft, grumpily heading home to their own wasted planet.

Avatar serves as a polemic against environmental injustice. But where does this film leave human beings? Quite literally *up in the air*. In *Avatar* humans are neither consciously nor conscientiously entangled with a planetary ecosystem—they are left in outer space. Humans are cut out of any multispecies entanglement, seen to be an almost purely parasitic species, a para-species worth keeping at bay. We must say *almost* because the main character played by Sam Worthington in fact ends up converting to the mindset—indeed to the *bios*—of the native people. In a way, then, the film functions as an environmental prophesy: the lesson is that after considering a variety of lifestyle choices, one can *choose* to be more intentionally entangled or not. Of course, this assumes that humans could *ever* be outside of what Timothy Morton, in *The Ecological Thought*, has called "the mesh" (28). The truth is far messier, and that brings us back to airportness.

"Turtles Invade Runway." This was a dramatic AOL headline in July 2009, when one afternoon 78 diamondback terrapin turtles crawled from the brackish water of Jamaica Bay and onto the tarmac at New York's JFK airport. Consequently flights were delayed for several hours, as ground crews herded the turtles and removed them from the runways and taxiways. It was a rare but not unprecedented incident, as it turns out that Jamaica Bay is a rich breeding ground for this kind of turtle, and the mass movement from water to land is a normal part of the ecosystem. But the humans in this ecosystem did not like being reminded of their entanglement with another species: the turtles were (re) routed, and planes soon took to the sky again. In a way, it was as if the fantastic scene in *Avatar* had already occurred, in mundane everyday life—but in this case, the humans simply brushed the animals aside and went about their business. Whereas *Avatar* distinguished rigorously between the moon Pandora (including its native people and animals) and the Other species (the humans), the JFK turtle takeover blurred such boundaries between the so-called natural world and human culture.

One view of this incident might emphasize the starkness of human control, exercised bluntly and swiftly against a discretely natural realm. From the standpoint of *Avatar*, this would have looked like a tragic win for the domineering human culture. But another perspective would show this as evidence that humans have their own organic logic of force and dissemination— as disturbing as it might be to think of it this way. From this perspective, the "turtles on the runway" incident at JFK serves as a more helpful "environmental" tale than *Avatar*, as it demonstrates the inescapable entanglement of humans in the ecological mesh—even as humans (falsely) assert their independence from the ecosystem. Whatever we (decide to) do, we nevertheless act as an elaborate species-function in an intricate mix, and thus the JFK airport delay should remind us of our complex place in the world: we are always interacting with other creatures, things that do *not* fit in a grid—cannot be plucked out as if from a Google image search. And even when in flight, we are flying through a biosphere—*itself in flight*—that is indifferent to our manic schedules. Those turtles may very well come back to haunt us.

The volcanic cloud of April 2010 that issued forth from Iceland and wafted over Europe marked another ominous reminder of our entanglements, via flight. First, the ash cloud was a news item: people were stranded at airports, flights were cancelled—it was the story of the hour. Humans found themselves in a predicament, working to disentangle themselves as quickly as possible. Second, the ash cloud hovered as what Don DeLillo might have called an "airborne toxic event" (*White Noise* 1986: 114) as significant as it was ephemeral, as encompassing as it was invisible (to most). In short, the ash cloud quickly became everyday life—it was (and now is) the space around us, the feelings of distance and proximity that make us anxious, expectant, eager, and uncertain. There was no locating the ash cloud, precisely— the more you looked for it, the more it disappeared. But at the same time, it was everywhere, and constantly being remediated by *us*. Consider how the ash cloud was compared obliquely to an indisputably human constructed event: as a *New York Times* article at the time put it, it was the worst disruption of air travel *since 9/11*. In the article one stranded passenger, a Hong Kong businessman, put it succinctly as such: "It's a natural issue. Never complain. You can't change this" ("Air Travel Crisis Deepens as Europe Fears Wider Impact"). Here is the nature of flight, laid bare: airportness as a *natural* issue.

Being entangled is not a choice, but it does require choices. We may not be able to change the outcomes or inevitabilities of volcanic events, exactly—but what *can* we change? We sometimes seem to forget that humans invented our means of flight. Humans also invented the idea of "environment." These are things we can change. Taken seriously, environment is not just that thing we fly through—it is what we eat, what we breathe, and what grounds us, too. In a sense, *we* are environment. This is what the birds and turtles show us, and jetBlue and Lufthansa, too.

The environment isn't a simple thing, and it's never simply an "issue." Environment means being entangled, every day—and it is no more and no less than the experience of *time*. The curiosities of air travel might teach us that environment is less about *space*, and more about *time*. Time is what we try to save when we fly. But there's no receptacle for time saved, no container for captured time. This is an uncanny awareness: you can't get out of time, and you can't save it. Perhaps instead of bumper stickers that say SAVE THE EARTH, we should wear T-shirts that say DON'T SAVE TIME. For in addition to planes and birds, bumper stickers and T-shirts are two other timely objects entangled with the nature of flight, or our unique patterns of migration and display.

Bodies shift and breathe around me—rows and rows of these bodies like mine in flight. Airportness is how we conform to these patterns, how we bend our bodies and our minds around the habits and procedures of plane life.

In-flight Entertainment III: *United 93*

Okay, okay—too much deep thinking. It's time to zone out again. Back to the screen gaping at me a few inches from my face. But wait, here's a peculiar in-flight movie on offer: *United 93*. Who on Earth made this apocryphal choice? Who wants to be reminded of the drama of 9/11 in flight, in real time?

And yet when I consider the increasingly meta-discursive and satirical safety briefing videos of Delta these days, or the tongue-in-cheek antics of Southwest flight attendants, the movie choice seems less outlandish: it is expected that everyone is always already in an ironic state of mind. Seeing the movie play out in disjointed scenes over few screens in front of me, as passive passengers flip around between programs and shows, I am put in a philosophical mood.

Among other problems that preoccupied him, the nineteenth-century German philosopher Friedrich Nietzsche struggled to understand how humans perform essentially as actors, playing elaborate roles based on intricate networks of fictions that accrete into truths—in other words, how humans function as creative subjects who convert everyday improvisations into firm realities. Can we ever become objectively aware of our reliance on the fabricated truths through which we live our lives? Would such awareness lead to enlightened being, or madness? Is it simply the case that to get by on a day-to-day basis, we will always be haunted by a nagging sense that living requires certain epistemological blind spots? In his essay "On Truth and Lying in a Non-moral Sense," Nietzsche wonders, "What do human beings really know about themselves? Are they even capable of perceiving themselves in their entirety just once, stretched out as in an illuminated glass case?" (142). The implicit answers to these questions seem to be that humans know very little about themselves; and, no, humans cannot perceive themselves in their entirety, "as in an illuminated glass case."

Yet Nietzsche himself glimpses an unsettling total vision, of sorts, in his stringent critique of truth later on in the same essay: "What, then, is truth? A mobile army of metaphors, metonymies, anthropomorphisms, in short, a sum of human relations which have been subjected to poetic and rhetorical intensification, translation, and decoration, and which, after they have been in use for a long time, strike a people as firmly established, canonical, and binding" (146). Given this assessment of truth, how do we proceed to live according to conventions that we know are fictions—particularly when we must come to terms with a certain event's truth, and our roles in making this truth— how else to put it—come true?

Some might contend that *cinema vérité* offers a unique way to view human life in its entirety, as if "in an illuminated glass case"—if only for ninety minutes or so—but I don't think this is exactly what Nietzsche had in mind. Whatever is happening around me as people casually watch *United* 93 and munch on miniature pretzels, it doesn't exactly resemble deep philosophical reflection.

Nevertheless the director of the film, Paul Greengrass, perhaps unintentionally rejuvenates Nietzsche's musings about how people might become aware of playing themselves amid "a sum of human relations" that we call truth. This film recreates the events of 9/11, specifically to dramatize the final hijacking that day aboard the eponymous United 93. To make this film, Greengrass cast many nonactors who play themselves in their roles as ordinary, unwitting laborers on the day of 9/11. That is, the movie includes many actual, professional workers who willingly recreated the roles that they played on September 11, 2001.

In the director's commentary on the DVD, Greengrass articulates his project, and his claims on behalf of real people, re-creation, and nonprofessional actors raise a series of problems and questions. Let's put some pressure on the idea of real people playing themselves. What is at stake in Greengrass's conception of a cinema that can get closer to the lived truth of the everyday? What does it actually mean to be able to *play* oneself, to desire to re-create a past moment on the screen (indeed, for the sake of entertainment)? Here is part of Greengrass's commentary:

> It was important to me that this film seemed to be about people who were just like anyone of us . . . part of the idea of 9/11 is that it is an event that engulfed US . . . it didn't belong to a rarified world of movie stars . . . it belonged in the everyday, in the here and now . . . [the presence of

professional air traffic controllers] gives this scene a special veracity . . . because . . . in the end . . . who better to play air traffic controllers . . . who better to bring this thing to realistic screen portrayal than professional people themselves?

Consider this: a film that seems to be about people "just like anyone of us"—that is, a film that doesn't even come off as a film, but as life itself. How would we even recognize ourselves as audiences to such a mundane show? This seems to be an awkward imperative, to live as if one's life is routinely insignificant—yet also always harboring a potential for spectacular cinematic truth. Greenwood's "rarified world of movie stars" is differentiated from the everyday; but isn't it precisely this rarified world that *does* occupy audiences every day, in cinemas around the world? On this plane right now, I see around me a surreal swirl of just this admixture: the majestically cinematic and the profoundly *un*spectacular. Can we actually pull apart these two "worlds" as if they are distinct? Finally, where is the "here and now" of flight United 93? This airline-specific designator has been engulfed by the aura of filmmaking: it has been re-spectacled within a double frame of serious entertainment. Have the particulars of this flight been made more real or less real—or differently real— by its having been simulated for the screen? And how do these professionals, these nonactors, contribute to such a reality shift?

Strangely, we are not too far from one of the commonly overheard responses to the actual events of 9/11, when people responded to the World Trade Center explosions with the incredulous observation: "It was just like a movie."

Indeed, *United 93* does not hesitate to recycle the recorded real-time perception—as well as its mediatization—of this filmic moment. At one point in the movie, when the second World Trade Center tower is hit, Greengrass uses "real" news footage from 9/11 to recapture from the expressions of real people ("who were there") the disbelief and alarm in the New York air traffic control tower and in the military command center. One shot fills up a good portion of the screen with the CNN footage, replete with the familiar, commanding red logo in the bottom right-hand corner of the screen (see Figure 21).

I am not critiquing the merits of Greengrass's filmmaking, nor am I trying to whip up the arguably controversial status of these clips. Rather, I am intrigued by the conception of human life forwarded by such images. What is this film saying about what it means to be a human? Are we being called upon to realize just how enmeshed we are in a "society of the spectacle," as Guy Debord called it? Or does this film get even more

Figure 21 United 93, © *2006 Universal Pictures International, directed by Paul Greengrass.*

tangled up as it tries to puncture the surface of images with the sharpness of the really real? The layers of mediation are dense and interpenetrating. And yet, they also get so easily absorbed back into the rhythms of uneventful air travel. Airportness is this delicate play between dullness and alertness in flight, between hyper-awareness and plain zoning out.

At another point in the director's commentary, Greengrass explains his goal for this film this way: "[If we] could create a film that allowed an audience to walk through 9/11 . . . at eye level . . . that would give us some basis for evaluating this enormously important event." Greengrass's idea of walking through 9/11 "at eye level" is fascinating, given our geographic displacements and replacements throughout the film: in Newark airport, in the flying plane, and in multiple air traffic control rooms and military command centers along the East Coast. While the camera angles are, in effect, positioned at eye level, and often handheld, the overwhelmingly significant comportment of 9/11 is not perambulation—it is the mechanical action of *flight*. This is a film about airportness. And, on another level, the salient aspect of this film is precisely the technical reproducibility of video. *United 93* exists for us to evaluate the Event; yet, as we have seen, part of the event was its non-exceptionality on many fronts—it was just another day at the office that became increasingly chaotic, while also increasingly subject to video recording.

This complex arrangement calls to mind one of Walter Benjamin's observations in his famous essay "The Work of Art in the Age of Mechanical Reproduction":

By close-ups of the things around us, by focusing on hidden details of familiar objects, by exploring commonplace milieus under the ingenious guidance of the camera, the film, on the one hand, extends our comprehension of the necessities which rule our lives; on the other hand, it manages to assure us of an immense and unexpected field of action. (236)

United 93 carries out these twin movements in spectacular form. On the one hand, the film explores "the commonplace under the ingenious guidance of the camera"—for instance, Greengrass used a pulley system to move the camera up and down the aircraft aisle to achieve a fluid, eye-level effect. We see the "hidden details" of the cockpit, the galley, and even the lavatory when the would-be hijacker constructs a (simulated) fake bomb above the toilet. The film "extends our comprehension of the necessities which rule our lives"—so not only is the everyday exposed, but it is also reinforced, normalized, and accepted as such. But this is not so much even in the content of the film as it is in the idea of what it means to *act* like ourselves. Thus the film also assures us of the "immense and unexpected field of action" that we call everyday life—the movie heightens our expectation for drama even as it insists on the banal ongoing march of progress.

What does one hope to achieve by seeing "real" people in the place of actors? What does one get from having the Event of 9/11 essentially compromised by its own representation, that is, reproduced in such a way that we can watch how it really must have felt, how it really happened? Not only that, but we can watch this film over and over, being reassured of its reality—its

Event-ness. It can even become another way to kill time on a commercial flight. For whom can 9/11 become such an Event, and what types of *events* are at play here?

This brings us back to Nietzsche, albeit in a roundabout way. One of Nietzsche's aphorisms from *Beyond Good and Evil* perplexes me every time I think about it: "Human maturity: this means rediscovering the seriousness we had towards play when we were children" (62). One possible way of reading this is as a joyous prompt to remain childlike even when an adult: I act the most mature when I am purely playful, inventive, maybe even silly. Another reading, however, mocks the very notion of human maturity: it is no *more* than what we felt years ago when we were children playing seriously in the sand—as adults we just have that same feeling in air traffic control rooms, in military command centers, and on airplanes. We call it maturity, but it is more like a forgetfulness of who and where we are, and what we are doing in any given moment. And a lot of these moments are taken up by work.

As we see consistently throughout *United 93*, one of the things that 9/11 variously interrupted and highlighted was *work*. 9/11 heightened the sense that what people were working for— wages, vacations, mobility, family, work itself—was suddenly on pause, and in certain cases violently threatened. The nonactors in *United 93* show us this through their acting. Yet understood as such, does acting *show* us the really real of work, or *is* it the really real of work? Paul Greengrass stresses that there is "a special veracity" in this film. I wonder if the truth of *United 93* is nothing more and nothing less than *work* itself: everyone's job is to *act professional.* The film *United 93* almost seems to rephrase Nietzsche's aphorism as such: human maturity consists in finding the seriousness one has as an *actor,* at work. We are left with the problem of playing ourselves, whether on the screen in lights, or in the darkening real of everyday life.

On this plane now, I wonder about all the intersecting and parallel lines of work and play, and how we are all struggling to keep these lines in order, even as they tangle and unspool like so many contrails crisscrossing the sky.

Old Planes

The first plane I was on today was new; this one is older, probably built in the early 1990s. It is a Boeing 757, a model first entering service in 1983 and with 738 planes still in service as of the time I write this. It cannot help but remind me of Donald Trump's signature private plane, also a 757, with its gold-plated fixtures and every onboard detail shrouded in luxury. Airplanes lead double lives, or multiple lives, carrying not only heavy baggage but heavy meanings, and always on the verge of going somewhere else—in our minds as well as across the ground and through time.

For instance, it's no coincidence that the same week that a *Wall Street Journal* article reported findings concerning air rage, or bad behavior by passengers in flight, there was also an uncontained engine failure on a Boeing 767. The 767 was developed concurrently to the 757; these are the two models of planes that were hijacked on 9/11. They are bound together in what Donna Haraway might call a "spiral dance" ("A Cyborg Manifesto" 1991: 181). Concerning the recent engine failure, a *Guardian* article mentioned in passing that the airliner in question is "from the 1980s or 1990s" and that the engine type, a General Electric CF6, has been in service for "decades" ("Plane engine fire prompts investigation at Chicago's O'Hare airport" 2016). One of the aggravating tricks of the trade seems to be the overhauling and revamping of old planes, squeezing more seats into cabins and improving the onboard Wi-Fi, while yet relying on fundamental flying technology that is quite aged.

Even if the parts are updated regularly, and pilots and ground crew carry out inspections meticulously, there nevertheless can be a sort of collective, sinking feeling about the worn state of flight. This is arguably what Donald Trump was tapping into during the first presidential debate in September 2016, when he railed against American airports as being "like from a third world country." He meant not just the physical interiors of airports, but everything from the vast infrastructure of air traffic control and runways to the amenities in terminals as well as the planes themselves lined up on the tarmac. Airportness is the unconscious awareness of old planes accreting, and that while they may get new paintjobs and better internet service, they are fundamental reminders of the tapering off of progress. It is no small irony that Trump's own iconic 757 is itself a relatively old plane, built in 1991, similar to this very aircraft I am on right now, but decked out to posh extremes, inside. That plane, with its oblique initial *T* slashing across the tail, flying fast, is still reliant on the gritty ground-level operations of refueling, human waste removal, and all the rest.

Driving around northern Michigan in the fall of 2016 before the election, I would look at the many dark blue TRUMP/PENCE signs stuck in yards and on hillsides by the road, and I would wonder what people imagined would change so definitively and abruptly in the case of Trump's projected presidency. By the time this book is published, we are finding out. But in those days, it occurred to me that airportness lingered around these signs, each one of them echoing Trump's private plane, each sign carrying the hopes and dreams of private mobility and fabulous wealth . . . while structurally tethered to a ground that is often messy, stuck in place, and not so easy to make "great" in any easy or quick way—"again" or no. Old planes and all the routines of our modernity will continue to haunt us for some time, unless something changes radically—something that we haven't anticipated, yet. What are the possible futures of our old planes? Are we up to the task of imagining a positive repurposing of airplanes and airports, possibly after the end of these things as we now know them? I hope so, perhaps against all odds.

Gender

If you've ever been consternated over the trouble with gender and public bathrooms, you might look to the heavens. You're not looking for a divine answer, though. Rather, gaze at all the airliners cruising by 35,000 feet above, contrails dissipating in the ether. They've got this issue figured out, more than you might think.

Gender in flight is not a problem. Airplane lavatories are non-gendered, and this works just fine, flight after mundane flight, day in and day out. Gender does not determine whether or not a person can fly a plane, or pass out pretzels. When it comes to your pilot, you probably care more about skills and training than what body parts they appear to have under their uniforms. Likewise with flight attendants: we have long since learned to care less about whether they present as male or female, and instead we care about whether they are snarky or sincere, miserly or generous, negligent or professional.

When a flight attendant asks passengers sitting in an exit row whether they are willing and able to help in the event of an emergency, this has nothing to do with gender, and everything to do with technical fluency, mental wherewithal, and physical ability. When it comes to facilitating an efficient evacuation, gender is not a critical factor—and we all accept this each time we take a commercial flight. Then think of your seatmate. It matters less if they seem to be a man or woman than if they are an armrest hog, an endless talker, or are donning an overpowering aroma.

There are endless differences that matter on an airplane, differences that make the gender binary little more than an incidental marker—and one that doesn't really matter beyond mere display. To paraphrase the philosopher Judith Butler, gender is more an *incredible* thing than a sure sign of credibility, one way or the other (*Gender Trouble* 2006). Genders can impress us, astonish us, confuse us, or simply fade into the background.

Airplanes are performance spaces where we actually, for the most part, just let genders *be*. Though sometimes limits are transgressed and enforced, even among the clouds: passengers wear the wrong clothes and get tossed off the plane, only to take out their anger online, via social media.

It is somewhat ironic that while we might think of airplanes as the most egregious sites for the recognition and policing of certain identities (terrorists being the obvious specter here), in other ways air travel also shows how little invested we are in patrolling other as-if absolute differences, such as gender.

Gender is usually less pressing and more slippery than its current hype would have us believe. Our airplanes can teach us that when it comes to people, there are almost always *more* differences than just two, and that being attuned to this *more* is what actually allows us to travel together in the first place.

Water Landing

As we begin our initial descent, I look down to see a stream meandering below, running from a dark spot of woods into a small lake. This flight is mostly over land, making the water evacuation instructions on our emergency briefing cards seem unnecessary, even a bit absurd. Flight attendants often make fun of this quirk in standardized rhetoric, mocking the "extremely unlikely" event of a water landing on *this* flight, as they go through their safety demonstrations.

Looking down at this stream I am reminded of a little adventure I went on with my son, in the woods behind our summer home in northern Michigan. There is a natural spring deep in the forest near our home, which comes burbling up through the sand within a grove of birch and hemlocks, and where sometimes we find frogs. When I tell my son Julien about this spring one day, he is excited to go look for a frog and bring one home. He asks for a bucket, but I can't find one—however, I tell him we can go on a scouting trip. He grudgingly approves, and so we head off into the valley. It's a long walk, a half-mile or so between high ridges and through steep valleys. We're traversing a landscape cut by glaciers. An Airbus A380 passes overhead; I point out the four widening contrails behind and the unlikely girth of the plane even at 35,000 feet, far above.

Halfway to the spring, we discover a gray five-gallon plastic bucket resting on its side next to an aspen tree. It is paint-smeared and disgusting, having been abandoned by some deer hunter, perhaps. But no matter its dubious provenance, it is a wish unexpectedly granted and Julien is ecstatic. So I grab the gnarly handle and take it along with us, and now we are really going on a frog hunt.

As we approach the spring I point out the differences between white, red, and scotch pines, and then I explain how my younger sister and brother used to try to clear out this spring to let it run free as a small creek through the valley. Alas, the trickle is so slight that it inevitably seeps into the sandy soil before being able to set a course into a proper stream, even with help.

When we arrive at the spring, its iron holding tank is partially covered with downed tree limbs, and clogged with leaves, muck, and debris. We spend thirty minutes or so clearing out oak leaves and other detritus from the old rusted cistern, until the dirt settles and we see the eyes of a bullfrog emerge through the surface of the tea-colored water. After a few botched attempts, we manage to scoop up the frog. We break off a chunk of birch limb and wedge it in the bucket at an angle, so that the frog can climb out of the water once he adjusts to his newfound captivity. I'm feeling slightly conflicted at this point, taking this frog away from its rather remote, pristine locale. But I try to remember Helen Macdonald's *H Is for Hawk*, concerning the vicissitudes of who is capturing whom—"the wild can be human work" (8)—and we begin the trip home with our newfound companion species.

As we tromp through a clearing, bracken fern up to our knees, the frog finally climbs uncertainly out onto the little log. He crouches there, swaying with the rhythm of the swinging bucket as we ramble on. Julien looks down at the frog, passenger on its part-log, and in a flash of insight he remarks: "It's like he's in an airplane!"

And this is airportness, the nature of flight: how my son was able to translate our experience of flying in airplanes onto another creature, soaring in a similar craft. He saw the frog being transported above ground, flying parallel to the surface of the Earth, removed to another station, and he drew an equivalence between his own experience of flight and the frog's current condition.

Sure, the frog's journey was involuntary and ad hoc—but then, how many humans have had an experience of involuntary flight, whether consciously or not? I think of Alison Kinney's speculative recounting in "Hostages" (2016) of her being spirited away from Korea to the United States as an infant, an adoptee unknowingly experiencing the pinnacle of flight, modern human migration at its finest, feeding desires and breaking bounds untold. Less literally, I think of the countless everyday travelers who at least by appearance seem swept along by the variable currents of flight, hardly in control as they fidget in their seats and queue up to pay exorbitant fees for bottled water and magazines at the airport newsstand.

When Julien makes the impromptu analogy between our bucket-riding frog and being in an airplane, he is not only conjuring the basic experience of airborne travel, but also channeling nuances and subtleties of the phenomenology of flight. The uncanny feeling of being pushed back in one's seat as the plane first gains momentum on the runway; the way the body tenses automatically to find equilibrium on the newfound "ground" of the plane; the eerie knowledge of land unfurling below (whether or not it is actually seen); the gut roil of turbulence—these are all witnessed in miniature in our frog who balances on the log, riding through the air a foot or so off the ground.

Back at home, Julien observes the frog for an hour or so, and shows it to his younger sister. Eventually the frog gets its bearings to the point where it hops up onto the lip of the bucket, ready to escape this confining, once airborne vessel. This too is a recognizable part of the nature of flight: what we call "air rage" is often simply a misplaced desire to *just get off the plane*, after one has been stuck in these close quarters for too long. Think back to the Millennium Falcon in *Star Wars*: it is called pejoratively a "bucket of bolts," and Princess Leia constantly wants to get out of it, when she's on it. But it's also the craft that saves her (as well as the other ragtag space heroes), again and again. Again, this pseudo-airliner contains a basic fact of airportness: it is the strong ambivalence of containment, or the queasy nature of flight. Our frog, too, has been encircled in airportness for long enough.

We pile into our car with the bucket and drive the frog down to where the spring reappears in a cedar swamp close to Lake Michigan after a mile of underground passage. Having found a suitable habitat for our temporary pet, I tip the bucket and send mud, log, and frog into the fen—an unlikely water landing for our amphibious passenger, and an end to its cross-country journey.

I'm jarred out of this memory as the plane tilts further into its decent. Out the window, more small lakes and rivulets intermix with patches of green, occasional roads weaving across the land. A water landing, while certainly unlikely here, would also be entirely possible, if not exactly successful. Perhaps this is really why flight attendants joke about the remote chance of this, at the beginning of a cross-country flight, and why passengers duly chuckle in response. Humor reroutes and represses the reality that it is always possible that an airplane might crash into a pond at precipitous speed, not unlike David Bowie's alien at the beginning of *The Man Who Fell to Earth*, or into a river like Chesley Sullenberger's US Airways Flight 1549, that miracle on the Hudson, that exception that proved the rule by breaking it.

The nature of flight is its openness to landing in water, however remote the possibility may seem. However high we have climbed as a species, we're also not too far away from just climbing out of the water.

Arrival

When our plane comes to a halt at the gate and a single "ding!" releases us from our seats, we stand, crouch, and jostle restlessly—this is one of the awkward moments of flight that can feel incredibly drawn out. How does it feel to you, to have to wait like this, when you're so close to the end?

I look around and see people fiddling with their bags and phones, or practicing micro-meditation exercises so as not to lose patience. The cabin becomes stuffy, as the internal air systems decelerate to barely a hiss. This is the time when seatmate friendships become embarrassing and forgotten, or are finally forged after hours of silence.

This is the time when excitement for what lies ahead, for who is waiting for you at baggage claim, can become nearly uncontainable. But this is also the time when existential dread can slam into the arriving passenger, hollow feelings of deep uncertainty concerning where one is, why one has come all this way, and what it all amounts to. And then there are all the feelings in between, reverberating in these concentrated minutes of arrival: fortifying oneself for a job ahead; logistical planning, figuring out how to get from airport to hotel; the exhale and simple relief to be back on the ground; gratitude for being home, almost.

Waiting, still waiting, for deplaning to begin in earnest.

Destination

While waiting, I steal one last glance out my window seat—taking stock of my destination, now that we're here. Forested hills line the horizon, above and beyond the airplanes and the jet bridges. My final destination lies beyond those hills; I can imagine it— even though, from where I'm sitting, the view basically resembles the vast sprawl of modernity at large. The destination of any air journey is always double: the unique place where you envision yourself, where you desire (or are desired) to be; and the generic terminal swirl of the airport, where everything bland and unseemly coalesces in an eddy. We are busy preparing to end this journey. But I am not done yet, and we're not done with airports yet: we can't leave them behind, but neither can we continue on with them in the state they are in. The idea of *destination* is an inescapable paradox, when it comes to airportness.

This time, especially, my destination carries another meaning: I am finally going to see Colin Farrell. (You didn't forget about him, reader, did you?) I look back from my seat, but cannot see him yet. There are too many people in the way.

People are finally moving, and I file as quickly as possible out of the plane and through the jet bridge. I cross the concourse quickly—to then turn around and set down my bag so that I resemble a passenger waiting to board. This little act of espionage seems ridiculously subversive, as I feign to be outbound rather than having reached my destination. I'm struck by how one can change roles so swiftly at airports, even when faking: I am now affecting the look of an outbound soul. I'm harmless, but still a little paranoid—conscious of my deception.

I watch my flight deplane, the suspense building.

I begin to notice faces familiar from the seats around the anointed row, and then . . . there he is.

But this isn't Colin Farrell at all.

It is a smaller, slightly dorkier version of Colin Farrell—maybe. He has the eyebrows and the complexion, perhaps, but . . . those aren't designer jeans, and they are too short, barely hitting his ankles. The polo shirt is a knockoff. What had appeared as sky blue on the plane is in fact an over-laundered, washed out aqua. I won't even mention the shoes.

He shuffles down the concourse, toting a faded JanSport backpack, and is soon absorbed by the masses converging onto a moving walkway, toward the arrivals area.

There had been no Colin Farrell on our airplane, all along. It was all fantasy, in my mind. The realization had probably rippled outward from his seat, disillusioning passengers one at a time, but, dampened by space and time, the truth never quite reached my row. I had been convinced the whole flight that he was there, in the air with me—I had felt a kind of vibration emanating from that seat. And yet . . . the reality was that it had been an utterly banal flight, no excitement to speak of, no celebrity sighting.

We have arrived at our destination, but it seems multiply abject. I feel utterly deflated and slightly embarrassed. All the possibilities of travel seem pathetic as I look around at the monotonous march of the airport. I am well aware that it is absurd to have become so wrapped up in this as-if celebrity sighting, but there's something here about the nature of flight that I have to tease out. Not in any rush to leave, I sit in an Eames Tandem Sling Seat and reflect.

I think back to the YouTube video of Björk attacking the journalist. What a stark contrast to my anticlimactic non-sighting of Colin Farrell. Still, it occurs to me that both of these scenes involve airportness. The stresses and pressures of flight become normal to us—*natural*—and we can intuit the body feel of air travel: the uncomfortable seats (in airports as well as in airplanes), long hurried walks to boarding gates, blaring screens, overpriced food, sterile lighting . . . how we learn to navigate the tight confines of the lavatory, or how we recognize an airport by the briefest clip in a film—a jet bridge, a waiting area, or a dank hallway through which a celebrity may be passing through, and might snap.

The spectral Colin Farrell on my plane caused the ordinary textures of the flight to become more vivid, if only for a few minutes: the layout of airline seating, the routines of beverage service, and the minutes and hours of an accepted paradox, jet propulsion that also feels bizarrely stationary.

In the case of Björk's Bangkok incident, the airport's ambient qualities were taken advantage of by the media personnel: they knew there would be bottleneck locations, perfect for photo ops and easily lobbed questions. Similarly, the walk from airliner to a presumably waiting vehicle was suffered by the singer, head down, a seeming tunnel of misery that couldn't be avoided, even by way of stardom. The airport is predictable, cognitively mappable—even in the way that Björk's outburst had to be contained, lest it become a security matter.

What these two incidents also share is a craving for a certain wildness: the chance of seeing a celebrity out in the rugged frontier of commercial flight. For all the regimented acts, security checks, and stern faces from airline personnel, air travel also becomes a deterritorialized realm, a rough space where the same old laws on the ground don't seem to apply. Just think of how spontaneous seatmate conversations can bloom; but, conversely, how you can simply ignore people and no one will think otherwise. Airspace is weird space, wild, with all the requisite sublime landscape views and a looming sense of the possibility of sudden, violent death.

Could we go as far as to say that air travel is a distinctly *Western* experience? This could be taken in several ways. It could be taken metaphorically to mean that flight is a sort of postmodern cowboy pursuit, wherein suit-clad businessmen ride the range of contemporary culture—how Walter Kirn treated air travel in his 2001 novel *Up in the Air*, with its frequent-flight obsessed, miles-gobbling main character; and how the television series *Mad Men* weaves the burgeoning of American commercial flight into its narrative.

But to call flight "Western" might also underscore it as a project aligned with colonization, manifest destiny, and hegemony. It is an unquestionable activity: it is accepted as a given that humans should fly. And thus, commercial flight acts as a sort of local status marker, and a semaphore for just how crappy any given political system is, from a Western standpoint.

Taken a third way, we might look at major Western airports—for instance, Denver International Airport, one of the few human-made things on Earth recognizable from space. From the vantage point of an airliner's window seat upon landing, the many-tented terminal building can be breathtaking, especially in certain lights. Echoing the Front Range of the Rockies, or perhaps some weathered outpost on the plains, the Denver airport invites surface associations with the long, uneasy histories of the American West. Inside and around the airport, more Western-themed art abounds.

It is not a stretch to imagine that an entire course on the American West could be taught in this airport—the subject matter is made explicit, reflected on overtly as well as subtly, and complexly entangled throughout the tunnels, tendrils, and tornado shelters of the vast structure. The airportness of this space is employed reflexively, to connect with broader themes and tensions that riddle the site. Whenever someone informs me that the Denver airport is associated with various conspiracy theories, I find myself pointing out that the airport is always already conspiring against itself. By which I mean that the Denver airport is teetering on a curious edge, always at pains to be a neutral, generic site of transfer while at the same time

working hard—architecturally, artistically, geographically—
to prompt humans to ponder questions of flight, mobility,
power, and history. The Denver airport, for all of its sprawl,
its problematically regular storms, and its almost absurd
dependence on moving walkways, is a model Western airport.
There are things here to be embraced and lingered on, and not
just haphazardly wished away. If we have arrived at some point
on our westward tilting journey, what is this endpoint, and
where are we going next? What would it mean to rally around
airports as a destination worth learning from, perhaps even to
be abandoned?

Baggage

Walking farther away from my gate now, shaking off the Colin
Farrell debacle and heading toward the NO RE-ENTRY signs, I
am bombarded by billboard-size ads for disparate things. You
may tune these out easily, if you are accustomed to such barrages
of media and advertising. But I notice two recurring motifs that
appear on the walls, in the halls: credit cards and luggage. The
credit card ads are often attached to airline loyalty programs.
And the airport proselytizes proper packing systems and proffers
glamorous luggage options, even as you trudge to retrieve your
own battered baggage. These two themes are often intermingled.

Since the rise of checked baggage fees in the first decades of
the twenty-first century, the airlines are keen to find ever more
opportunities to make free checked baggage seem like the most

sought after—and yet achievable—privilege. (No matter that this was standard operating procedure a mere fifteen years ago.) The most common tactic is the airline-affiliated credit card. If you have the card, you are allowed a certain number of checked bags at no extra cost.

One wall-size ad for a MileagePlus Explorer Chase Visa blares out such a message: "Going home for a long weekend, we'll save $100 with a **Free Checked Bag**." (See Figure 22.)

Figure 22 *MileagePlus Explorer Chase Visa.*

The final words are unnecessarily capitalized, calling to mind writing traditions from centuries prior, when capitalizing a word not only gave it emphasis but endowed it with a kind of spiritual weightiness, making something into an ideal form. The Free Checked Bag would appear to be our new Truth or Beauty: all we know on Earth, and all we need to know.

The ad shows a preppy white couple flashing their blue credit card and as-if causally connected gleaming smiles. Modest shoulder bags suggest that they are traveling unburdened. They await their Free Checked Bag, as evinced in the foggy background: a luggage chute with a number 3 at the top, and a suitcase tumbling down toward the revolving belt below. Off to the side, luggage carts are neatly lined up, ready to be rented for the long haul to the parking lot.

This is all plain enough, a simple ad for a credit card that will allow the savvy passenger to check a Free Bag. I get it. But I cannot help but fixate on the eerie, milky backdrop of the ad, with its unpeopled atmosphere and bleak reality. For how are we to interpret this space? With plenty of time now to linger in this space, I pause to consider.

The baggage claim area being empty means only one of two things: the couple could be the first to the claim, making them appear ahead of the crowd. But let's not be naïve: the MileagePlus Explorer card is no elite platinum card. Other, first class fliers would have beaten this couple to the claim—we might see them in the distance, suit-clad and checking their phones or standing with chauffeurs.

Our couple can't have beaten the entire plane to the baggage claim, either, as there is already a bag cascading onto the belt. In fact, noticeably, there is only *one bag*. More likely, then, our couple is *the last couple* from their flight, waiting in earnest for their Free Checked Bag—a bag that, very possibly, *has not arrived at all*. Their smiles do look a bit forced, after all. Forcibly smug. And whose bag is that, the one sliding down to the belt? Another lost bag, to be unclaimed in the present scene? Or perhaps that bag *is* the couple's bag, they just haven't spotted it yet . . . but if so, the scene nevertheless retains a disturbing insularity, an aura of isolation that is inconsistent with even the most effortless and smooth day of flight.

The journalist Nathan Heller once reviewed my earlier airport books, concluding that at times I seemed "a touch insane." Should he ever read this book, I can imagine Heller rolling his eyes as he reads my meditation on baggage, thinking I've gone off the rails again as I overanalyze this throwaway credit card ad in the name of my obsessive airport studies.

But how is the picture of this ad not a pathetic situation, this celebration of a Free Checked Bag in the dank waste space of the baggage claim? I am put in the mindset of the poet John Keats in "Ode on a Grecian Urn," wondering "What men or gods are these? What maidens loth? / What mad pursuit? What struggle to escape?"

Like it or not, airportness expresses itself as the pinnacle of our modern romance: it is where we go for adventures, how we measure self-worth, and where art is invested in by default.

This situation—the airport as our reflective urn—is hardly something to swoon over. Yet this is precisely what the MileagePlus Explorer card ad asks us to do, in name (Explore!) and in the romantic coupling intimated by the foreground. A

Free Checked Bag: is this enough for us to live on, a surrogate for something like love? Or is this just our collective baggage, a tattered container for frozen human ambitions?

Exit

In the non-sterile zone of the airport, family and friends wait for loved ones, and chauffeurs dutifully hold signs with names. It is an anxious space, this realm of transition within the airport, where you can pick up on the energy of long anticipated reunions: friends hiding behind a column to surprise their arriving comrade; a waiting lover with flowers, on tiptoes, grinning; a gruff-looking hillbilly in camouflage, who melts giddily upon seeing his grandchild stumbling out of the gate area, pulling a Dora the Explorer roller bag. But also the angry relative scowling into the deplaned passengers, shouting into a phone that they don't see them coming, nowhere. The jittery, shifty-eyed souls who are waiting for . . . who knows?

It's hard to do justice to these moments that bloom and dissipate each day at airports, presumably all around the world. You can pause to watch these fleeting interactions and stalwart comportments— or you can pass them by, knowing they'll happen again and again, any other day at the bittersweet end of the terminal.

Spat out back on the curbside, now veering away from the airport—the journey is done. Or is it? On the highway a few miles away, a distant roar from above and sure enough that is my plane, departing again and off to another destination. The airport follows me as I race away from it. I can't help but continue to think about it, and not just the airport, but the airports I've been through today, the airports that are still pulsating right now, not just those airports but *all* airports, a vast machine or even creature with innumerable tendrils.

What are airports, at their best, and at their worst?

At their best, airports are places of imagination, sites where the thrill of a voyage commingles with the humility of being one mortal among countless others in transit. Airports are places that can grant geographic knowledge, and even geologic perspective. Airports are liminal zones of suspense and unknowing—and realms of boredom, which can lead to contemplation. At their best, airports can be architectural marvels, inviting passengers and workers alike to consider what it actually means to inhabit space, to migrate, to breathe. Airports can showcase striking artworks, and can themselves be provocative pieces of art.

At their worst, airports are places of rampant control, sites where manic security and paranoia commingle with pompous self-regard and obliviousness to the fact of coexistence. Airports are an admixture of repression and expression, displaying at once extreme expenditures and parsimonious measures everywhere you look. At their worst, airports are despised, both in their everyday operations and in their general aura. Airports can be places that seem to disappear, even as their structures of status and networks of mobility proliferate and accrete.

What sort of airports, if any, will we choose for the future to come? How will airportness be remembered, what will be its legacy on our planet? Our trip is not over, not yet.

Home

I'm back home, at last. I feel the day of air travel fading away. Familiar things surround me; this is the antithesis of the airport.

But airportness continues to surround me, and draws me back into its aura. I can smell the air journey on my clothes. I'm not home for more than fifteen minutes when my phone buzzes: the airline has sent me a customer satisfaction survey, asking me to think back though my entire trip and rate each stage—reconsidering each airline worker along the way, each moment of transition, exchange, interaction.

A package is waiting for me on my stoop; the shipping label bears the three-letter codes of other airports, the journey it took to arrive here.

I dump out the contents of my bag and put travel-size amenities away in the bathroom, gauging which ones need to be replenished. Even these small shampoo and toothpaste tubes embody the spirit of airportness, anticipate another trip to come.

I nearly stumble over one of my daughter's toys on the floor, a Lego "Friends" airplane. Its rear ceiling panel is ajar, and I see her mini-figure "Olivia" sitting on the toilet in the miniature lavatory, an eager grin on her face and the familiar confines boxing her in.

The simple if elusive lesson of this book is that airportness transcends airports themselves, and reaches not only into airplanes but also out into everyday life, far beyond the terminal buildings. It has just as much to do with surface-level features, such as sloping hallways and undulating rooflines, as with a host of more disparate effects that make air travel something modern humans have internalized and learned to live with.

I glance at my phone and follow a notification to my Twitter feed, and immediately see people reporting on myriad facets of flight: complaining about overhead bin space, celebrating an on-time arrival, capturing a cloudscape at once common and sublime. This is an ongoing, minor epic: the air journey writ large, and dispersed among countless travelers. One tweet by Nathan Jurgenson reads:

"hi adult, eat here. fuck you." -airports #postdignitydesign

The tweet includes a picture of four loosely aligned, small, standing tables where passengers can presumably eat; foot rests are attached about six inches off the ground, as if to offer a modicum of reprieve from the hustle of flight. The tweet insinuates that airports interpellate passengers into the adventure of flight, only to subject them to banal and dehumanizing indignities, such as eating a hurried meal standing up. This too is airportness as a general language: the material example of these grim stand-up feeding stations allows us to give voice to a common sentiment involving air travel. And the tweet is jokingly signed, as if written by "airports"—as if the space speaks through its furniture, even via an ironic tweet, to get at some spoken truth.

And this is not always a matter of cynical realism. Such attention to detail can also make airports seem endearing, familiar, even charming. Take the carpet in Portland's airport, otherwise known as "PDX carpet," which has become a subcultural phenomenon complete with active hashtags, a cottage industry of similarly patterned products for sale (socks, pillows, microbrew bottles, etc.), and a loose social media custom wherein passengers share photos of themselves standing on the carpet with their shoes peeking into the frame. The PDX carpet is a comforting, kitschy piece of airportness, a shared experience that mediates and literally subtends the extreme act of air travel for passengers passing through that terminal. But moreover, the singularity of PDX carpet is made possible by the fact of airport carpets and airport codes as general aesthetic forms, first. We recognize the vast sweeps of airport carpets and comprehend the three-letter locator codes of air fields, and these aspects of airportness allow the specific site of Portland to become an internet meme, flying in the face of place.

Mark Vanhoenacker defines "place lag" as the palpable and disorienting sense of geographical difference made possible by long-haul jet travel. In an article for the *Guardian* titled "Why I love being a pilot," he likens it to jet lag:

> Nobody enjoys jet lag, of course, but time zones do serve to remind us of a fact so fundamental we rarely consider it—that the world is round and turning slowly in the light of a star. In the same way, place lag reasserts the fascinating differences that persist across the world even in this age of globalization. To encounter such differences, of course, is the main reason people travel.

For Vanhoenacker, place lag offers opportunities for humility, reflection, and genuine connection with difference—even while it has an equal capacity to confuse and humiliate. Place lag is a quintessential aspect of airportness, capturing the thrill associated with long flights and exotic destinations that then also makes them somewhat interchangeable in all their potential for excitement and exhaustion.

As we've seen, this complex ambivalence is called upon each time an international airport terminal appears in a film, even in the briefest of scenes, to conjure the surges of travel and the romantic possibilities of flight. And it can be miniaturized, and made simulacral, as the description of the Lego City Airport Passenger Terminal building kit suggests:

> Catch a flight from LEGO® City to anywhere! Pack your bags and get ready to go on vacation! Head to the airport and check in at the terminal. Put your luggage on the conveyor belt and watch it get loaded onto the passenger airplane. Go through security and then head out the revolving doors to the loading area. Climb the stairs and get buckled in, your trip is about to start!

The minutiae and otherwise dull procedures of airport passage are here hyperbolized (go *anywhere*?) and made extraordinary: baggage becomes exciting, even a spectacle. The tedious routines of flight—revolving doors, check-in, security, waiting—are yoked with the rhetorical uplift of anticipated place lag and packaged so that children can experiment with airportness at a young age.

There's also the Lego City Airport VIP Service building kit, which carries quite different connotations:

Travel to your next business meeting in style! Make sure you have all your important papers packed and ready! Help the pilot get the private plane ready for the next client, who should be arriving shortly. Drive the businesswoman to the airport in the limousine and make sure she gets to her plane on time. Take a seat and buckle up—it's time for takeoff!

In this toy story, which cannot help but evoke the specter of Donald Trump and his ultra-wealthy ilk, airportness is a minimal trace, held at bay—something that the elite spirit through, shrouded in luxury. Again, the set's description is littered with exclamation marks, but mysteriously here the subject position shifts around from the very important passenger, to the pilot, to the limo driver, and back to the business traveler. It is almost as if this airport toy, which overtly seeks to minimize the airport experience (for the elite traveler) in fact exposes the fact that the complex labor of flight cannot be so easily elided.

Airportness is always in dynamic relation to the elaborate infrastructures and economic flows that facilitate human flight, and just as Mark Vanhoenacker's book *Skyfaring* is attuned to multifaceted social and economic disparities around the world, children's model airports are no less enmeshed with the pressures and problems of globalization. Part of this book has involved my own attempts to understand (and, at times, play with) airport toys and representations as they have entered my children's lives. Airportness is not just the stuff of adults, as becomes all too obvious whenever there is an "unaccompanied minor" mix-up in the news, or if you have a particularly obnoxious or disconcerting child as a seatmate. (Another recent airport tweet reads, "Why does the kid seated next to me need to keep talking about fire?")

Airportness is how flight becomes natural to us, expected and accepted: contrails in the sky, layovers between flights, and the stuff of contemporary childhood. Just as I am finishing this book, my son brings me his reading homework, a book called *Where Is My Pet?* The first page asks, "Is my pet in the jet?" A smug frog lounges in a first class seat, in a thought bubble—the wondering boy holds a toy plane, and so much airportness gets bundled into a rudimentary reading lesson.

I find myself returning to Donald Trump's claims about American airports as awful places. Are our airports really *that* bad? Sure, there are the aggravating document checks on the ground, long walks through dank tunnels, and overpriced amenities—but they are also climate controlled, there's food available, and there are spots to sit down and plug in while busy workers labor to prepare aircraft for flight. Are these places really so atrocious? If so, why would we see them so readily exported into playthings? In his classic essay *A Supposedly Fun Thing I'll Never Do Again*, David Foster Wallace once wrote as an aside that the word "airport" denotes "a zone and not a thing" (271). Airportness is precisely this imprecise zone, this realm full of things and phenomena, and how our feelings for them get woven and twisted around.

Maybe what it so disturbing about airports is that they reflect the complexities and contradictions of this moment in history. Our worst tendencies run rampant at airports, but some of our most impressive achievements are also on display. Airports bring us together across vast geographic spaces, and yet they can tear us apart in scary ways (individually as well as collectively). Airportness is our current way of inhabiting the Earth, our movement and our destination. We're deeply entangled with airportness—and it's up to us to figure out what to do with it, how to live with the nature of flight.

We can have both direct and indirect impacts on airportness, but these impacts might not be what we anticipate or envision at the outset. Changing airportness might mean decreasing the number of airports, reducing flight paths over our country (and around the world). It might mean reinvesting in rail transport, or some other as yet unimagined mode of mass transit. Airportness will inevitably become a marker of the past; the question is, how do we embrace and proactively affect this particular timing of space, and its recession into the future?

When it comes to airports there is no going back to a "great" time—this is where we are, and we are inevitably moving forward, never backward. Moving forward, we may want to look closely at the contradictions that airports manage to hold together. Could some of the intricacies of airportness stand in for *Americanness*, even as this national appellation trembles on the brink of oblivion or progressive rebound? Are there things here we could accept and rally around at airports, even when they may seem repellent or difficult, at first blush? Is airportness something we might learn from, if then to revise and remake, for a future to come? Either way, there's no going back to a golden age of flight or to a land of pristine airports as a synecdoche of utopia. Airportness means being a hyperactive species in

Figure 23 *Airplane mode.*

motion. It might also become something we can look back upon, having learned from.

My phone buzzes again, alerting me to the arrival of an email receipt for something I bought at the airport. Tired of my phone's constant nagging, I attempt to silence it—only to be confronted with the nature of flight once more in the guise of "airplane mode," that little jetliner motif that reminds me that travel is always a thumb swipe away (see Figure 23). Even at home I'm always either in airplane mode, or not—as if there is no other option than to be in constant relation to airportness.

Acknowledgments

Thanks first to my editor Haaris Naqvi for believing that I could write a third book about airports. I'm grateful to the whole team at Bloomsbury, detail oriented and efficient at every turn. Thanks to my colleagues and students at Loyola University New Orleans; to my faithful research assistant Alana Demaske; to my department chair, John Biguenet, and my dean, Maria Calzada, for their ongoing support of my airport projects (and especially for supporting the sabbatical that allowed me to finish this book). Thanks to Ian Bogost and Kara Thompson for collaboration and friendship. Thank you Susan Clements for another elegant index. Thanks to my parents, Susann and Jim Schaberg, for providing space and time for me to write, read, and think in Michigan. Parts of this book were published in earlier forms at *The Atlantic*, *Invisible Culture*, *The New Inquiry*, *The Philosophical Salon*, *Public Books*, *Real Life*, *Resilience*, *Guernica*, and in the edited collection *Curious Collectors, Collected Curiosities: An Interdisciplinary Study*—thanks to all the editors who made my writing tighter and more coherent along the way. I'm very thankful to have Mark Yakich as a friend and book doctor: his edits and suggestions as the book came together were invaluable. Finally, thanks to my wonderful family—Lara, Julien, and Camille—for everything, and everything else.

Bibliography

Baldwin, James. *Giovanni's Room*. New York: Dial Press, 1956.

Ballard, J. G. *Super-Cannes*. New York: Picador, 2000.

Barthes, Roland. *Mythologies*. Translated by Annette Lavers. New York: Noonday, 1972.

Barthes, Roland. *Roland Barthes*. New York: Hill and Wang: 2010.

Barry, Kathleen. *Femininity in Flight: A History of Flight Attendants*. Edited by Daniel Walkowitz and Barbara Weinstein. Durham, NC: Duke University Press, 2007.

Barton, Byron. *Planes*. New York: HarperFestival. 1998.

Butler, Judith. *Gender Trouble: Feminism and the Subversion of Identity*. Routledge Classics. New York: Routledge, 2006.

Cohen, Jeffrey Jerome and Linda T. Elkins-Tanton. *Earth*. New York: Bloomsbury, 2017.

Davis, Lydia. "The Woman Next to Me on the Airplane." *Can't and Won't*. New York: Penguin, 2014.

Debord, Guy. *The Society of the Spectacle*. New York: Zone, 1994.

DeLillo, Don. *White Noise*. New York: Penguin, 1986.

DeLillo, Don. *Zero K*. New York: Scribner, 2016.

Dicum, Gregory. *Window Seat: Reading the Landscape from the Air*. San Francisco: Chronicle Books, 2004.

Fitzgerald, F. Scott. "Three Hours Between Planes." *Esquire*, July 1941.

Gomi, Taro. *Everyone Poops*. My Body Science Series. 3rd ed. Translated by Amanda Mayer Stinchecum. La Jolla, CA: Kane/Miller, 2001.

Haraway, Donna. "A Cyborg Manifesto: Science, Technology, and Socialist Feminism in the Late Twentieth Century." In *Simians, Cyborgs and Women: The Reinvention of Nature*, 149–81. New York: Routledge, 1991.

Hemingway, Ernest. *The Sun Also Rises: The Hemingway library Edition*. New York: Simon and Schuster, 2014.

Hillman, Brenda. "Symmetry Breaking," *Loose Sugar*. Hanover: Wesleyan University Press, 1997.

Jacobs, Dawn and Marion Elderidge. *Where Is My Pet?* Parsippany, NJ: Pearson, 2000.

Kinney, Alison. "Hostages (October 23–24, 1975)." In *Airplane Reading*, edited by Christopher Schaberg and Mark Yakich, 122–27. Winchester, UK & Washington, USA: Zero Books, 2016.

Kirn, Walter. *Up in the Air.* New York: Doubleday, 2001.

Lopez, Barry. "Flight," *About This Life: Journeys on the Threshold of Memory.* New York: Vintage, 1999.

Macdonald, Helen. *H Is for Hawk.* New York: Grove Press, 2016.

Mandel, Emily St. John. *Station Eleven.* New York: Vintage, 2014.

Morton, Timothy. *The Ecological Thought.* Cambridge, MA: Harvard University Press, 2012.

Nietzsche, Friedrich. "On Truth and Lying in a Non-Moral Sense." *The Birth of Tragedy and Other Writings.* Cambridge: Cambridge University Press, 1999.

Nietzsche, Friedrich. *Beyond Good and Evil.* Cambridge: Cambridge University Press, 2002.

Stevens, Wallace. "Thirteen Ways of Looking at a Blackbird." *The Palm at the End of the Mind.* New York: Vintage, 1990.

Tea, Michelle. *Black Wave.* New York: Feminist Press at CUNY, 2016.

Van Dooren, Thom. *Flight Ways: Life and Loss at the Edge of Extinction.* New York: Columbia University Press, 2014.

Vanhoenacker, Mark. *Skyfaring.* Vintage Departures. Reprint, New York: Vintage, 2016.

Wallace, David Foster. *The Broom of the System.* New York: Viking Press, 1987.

Wallace, David Foster. *A Supposedly Fun Thing I'll Never Do Again.* New York: Back Bay, 1998.

Wallace, David Foster. *The Pale King.* New York: Little, Brown & Co., 2011.

Walter, Benjamin. "The Work of Art in the Age of Mechanical Reproduction." *Illuminations.* New York: Schocken, 1969.

Whitman, Walt. "Song of Myself," *Leaves of Grass.* Philadelphia: David McKay Publications, 1900.

Films

Avatar. Directed by James Cameron. Los Angeles: 20th Century Fox, 2009.

Captain America: Civil War. Directed by Anthony Russo and Joe Russo. Burbank, CA: Walt Disney Studios Motion Pictures, 2016.

Dwelling. Directed by Hiraki Sawa. 2002.

Greengrass, Paul. "Feature Commentary with Director Paul Greengrass." Disc 1. *United 93*, widescreen ed. DVD. Directed by Paul Greengrass. Los Angeles: Universal Pictures, 2006.

Louie. "Travel Day/South." Created by Louis C. K. Los Angeles: FX, July 20, 2010.

Mad Men. Created by Matthew Weiner. New York: AMC. 2007–15.

Somewhere. Directed by Sofia Coppola. Universal City, CA: Focus Features, 2010.

Star Wars: The Force Awakens. Directed by J. J. Abrams. Burbank, CA: Walt Disney Studios Motion Pictures, 2015.

The Man Who Fell to Earth. Directed by Nicolas Roeg. London: British Lion Films, 1976.

Top Gun. Directed by Tony Scott. Los Angeles: Paramount Pictures, 1986.

United 93. Directed by Paul Greengrass. Los Angeles: Universal Pictures, 2006.

Web resources

"Airport Passenger Terminal." *LEGO Shop*. https://shop.lego.com/en-US/Airport-Passenger-Terminal-60104?mPageNo=2 (Accessed December 20, 2016.)

"Airport VIP Service." *LEGO Shop*. https://shop.lego.com/en-US/Airport-VIP-Service-60102 (Accessed December 20, 2016.)

Alter, Alexandra. "Rhapsody, a Lofty Literary Journal, Perused at 39,000 Feet." *New York Times*. May 3, 2015. http://www.nytimes.com/2015/05/04/business/media/rhapsody-the-in-flight-magazine-is-becoming-a-first-class-literary-journal.html (Accessed December 20, 2016.)

AOL.com Editors. "Turtles Invade JFK Airport, Cause Flight Delays." *AOL Lifestyle*. June 29, 2011. http://www.aolnews.com/story/turtles-invade-runway/562870 (Accessed December 20, 2016.)

Ballard, J. G. "Airports: The True Cities of the 21st Century." *The Utne Reader* online. http://www.utne.com/politics/homeiswherethehangaris (Accessed December 22, 2016.)

"Björk attacks a reporter." Online video clip. *Youtube*. February 20, 2006. https://youtu.be/W3mJTdGE79I (Accessed December 20, 2016.)

Blake, Aaron. "The First Trump-Clinton Presidential Debate Transcript, Annotated." *The Washington Post*. September 26, 2016. https://www.washingtonpost.com/news/the-fix/wp/2016/09/26/the-first-trump-clinton-presidential-debate-transcript-annotated/ (Accessed December 20, 2016.)

"Boeing 747 Plane crash in Bagram—Bagram 747 crash." Online video clip. *Youtube*. May 2, 2013. https://www.youtube.com/watch?v=-MB9JDBe4wA (Accessed December 20, 2016.)

Brody, Richard. "A Place for 'Somewhere.'" *The New Yorker*. December 15, 2010. http://www.newyorker.com/the-front-row/a-place-for-somewhere (Accessed December 20, 2016.)

Calabrese, Erin. "Alec Baldwin thrown off AA flight at LAX for 'playing game' on phone." *New York Daily News*. December 6, 2011. http://nypost.com/2011/12/06/alec-baldwin-thrown-off-aa-flight-at-lax-for-playing-game-on-phone/ (Accessed December 20, 2016.)

Chozick, Amy. "Hillary Clinton Unveils New Plane, and Lets Journalists On Board." *New York Times*. September 5, 2016. http://nyti.ms/2ciPFfd (Accessed December 20, 2016.)

"David Bowie – Blackstar." Online music video. *Youtube*. November 19, 2015. https://youtu.be/kszLwBaC4Sw (Accessed December 20, 2016.)

"David Bowie Interview Dick Cavett Show 1974 Part 2." Online video clip. *Youtube*. September 7, 2012. https://youtu.be/SPiocjOdQhY?t=1m2s (Accessed December 20, 2016.)

Dean, Jon. "Are Travellers Safe? From Istanbul to Glasgow and Brussels—10 airport attacks that shook the world." *Mirror*. June 29, 2016. http://www.mirror.co.uk/news/world-news/travellers-safe-istanbul-glasgow-brussels-8307934 (Accessed December 20, 2016.)

EileenMyles. "@airplanereading prob." April 2, 2016, 9:29 a.m. https://twitter.com/EileenMyles/status/716301649677930497 (Accessed December 20, 2016.)

Erlanger, Steven and Jack Ewing. "Air Travel Crisis Deepens as Europe Fears Wider Impact." *New York Times*. April 17, 2010. http://nyti.ms/1FpSWoe (Accessed December 20, 2016.)

Graham, David A. "How Trump's Abuse of Women Hid in Plain Sight." *The Atlantic*. October 13, 2016. http://www.theatlantic.com/politics/archive/2016/10/how-trumps-abuse-of-women-hid-in-plain-sight/503954/ (Accessed December 20, 2016.)

Heller, Nathan. "Air Head." *The New Yorker*. February 1, 2016. http://www.newyorker.com/magazine/2016/02/01/air-head (Accessed December 20, 2016.)

Keats, John. "Ode on a Grecian Urn." Poetry Foundation. https://www.poetryfoundation.org/poems-and-poets/poems/detail/44477 (Accessed December 20, 2016.)

Krieg, Gregory. "Sanders Flies Coach, Social Media says he's First Class." *CNN*. December 29, 2015. http://www.cnn.com/2015/12/29/politics/bernie-sanders-on-a-plane/ (Accessed December 20, 2016.)

Lee, Esther. "Watch Audi's Breathtaking Super Bowl 50 Commercial Featuring David Bowie's 'Starman.'" *US Weekly*. February 4, 2016, 2:19 p.m. http://www.usmagazine.com/celebrity-news/news/audis-super-bowl-50-ad-features-david-bowies-starman-watch-now-w163459 (Accessed December 20, 2016.)

Lynch, E. D. W. "Airplane Lavatory Self-Portraits in the Flemish Style." *Laughing Squid.* April 10, 2012. http://laughingsquid.com/airplane-lavatory-self-portraits-in-the-flemish-style/ (Accessed December 20, 2016.)

"Men's Air Strip™ Long Sleeve Shirt." *ExOfficio*. https://www.exofficio.com/products/details/mens-air-strip-long-sleeve-shirt (Accessed December 20, 2016.)

"Men's PFG Tamiami™ II Short Sleeve Shirt." *Columbia Sportswear*. http://www.columbia.com/mens-pfg-tamiami-ii-short-sleeve-shirt-FM7266.html (Accessed December 20, 2016.)

Nathanjurgenson. "'hi adult, eat here. fuck you.' -airports #postdignitydesign." September 5, 2016, 9:40 am. https://twitter.com/nathanjurgenson/status/772806642576527360 (Accessed December 20, 2016.)

Neate, Rupert. "Los Angeles Airport to Build Special Terminal just for Celebrities." *The Guardian*. November 19, 2015. https://www.theguardian.com/us-news/2015/nov/19/los-angeles-airport-celebrity-terminal-lax (Accessed December 20, 2016.)

Novak, Matt. "Trump Supporters Claim First Class Armrests Couldn't Move in the 1980s, Which Is a Lie." *Gizmodo*. October 13, 2016. http://gizmodo.com/trump-supporters-claim-first-class-armrests-couldnt-mov-1787749381 (Accessed December 20, 2016.)

Oosting, Jonathan. "Is Detroit Metro Airport going to the birds? Sparrow 'sanctuary' makes movie poster." *MLive*. May 24, 2010, 9:18 a.m. http://www.mlive.com/business/detroit/index.ssf/2010/05/is_detroit_metro_airport_going.html (Accessed December 20, 2016.)

Osipova, Natalia V. "'His Hands Were All Over Me.'" Online video clip. *New York Times*. October 12, 2016. https://www.nytimes.com/video/us/politics/100000004705688/his-hands-were-all-over-me-trump.html (Accessed December 20, 2016.)

"Our World." "INSTANT JUSTICE: Trump "Sexual Assault" Story Immediately Debunked With 3 Simple Photos—Subject: Politics." October 15, 2016. https://nackpets.wordpress.com/2016/10/15/instant-justice-trump-sexual-assault-story-immediately-debunked-with-3-simple-photos-subject-politics/ (Accessed December 20, 2016.)

Oxford English Dictionary. "lavatory, n." http://www.oed.com/view/Entry/106352 (Accessed December 20, 2016.)

"Patagonia Men's Long-Sleeved Island Hopper II Shirt." *Patagonia.* http://www.patagonia.com/product/mens-long-sleeved-island-hopper-ii-shirt/52181.html (Accessed December 20, 2016.)

Patterson, Thom. "Preventing another 'Miracle on the Hudson' emergency." *CNN.* September 12, 2016. http://www.cnn.com/2016/09/09/us/sully-sullenberger-miracle-hudson-bird-strike-prevention/ (Accessed December 20, 2016.)

"PLAYMOBIL Cargo and Passenger Aircraft." *Amazon.* https://www.amazon.com/PLAYMOBIL-Cargo-and-Passenger-Aircraft/dp/B0077QST58 (Accessed December 20, 2016.)

Quilty-Harper, Conrad. "The best advert of Superbowl 50 features David Bowie (of course)." *GQ.* February 7, 2016. http://www.gq-magazine.co.uk/article/superbowl-audi-r8-david-bowie (Accessed December 20, 2016.)

Rhapsody. January, 2016. http://ink-live.com/emagazines/united-rhapsody/2368/january-2016/#1/z (Accessed December 20, 2016.)

Samuel, Henry. "Gerard Depardieu 'sorry' to have Urinated on Plane Carpet." *The Telegraph.* August 17, 2011. http://www.telegraph.co.uk/news/celebritynews/8707789/Gerard-Depardieu-sorry-to-have-urinated-on-plane-carpet.html (Accessed December 20, 2016.)

Schaberg, Christopher. "On Style: Sofia Coppola's *Somewhere.*" January 6, 2011. http://whatisliterature.blogspot.com/2010/12/sofia-coppola-somewhere.html (Accessed January 9, 2017.)

Stewart, Amy. "Signs of Life at Denver International Airport." *Garden Rant.* January 21, 2008, 5:47 am. http://gardenrant.com/2008/01/signs-of-life-a.html (Accessed December 20, 2016.)

"Super Hero Airport Battle." *LEGO Shop.* https://shop.lego.com/en-US/Super-Hero-Airport-Battle-76051 (Accessed December 20, 2016.)

The Guardian. "Plane engine fire prompts investigation at Chicago's O'Hare airport." October 29, 2016. https://www.theguardian.com/us-news/2016/oct/29/chicago-plane-american-airlines-fire-investigation-ohare (Accessed December 20, 2016.)

The New York Times. "Air Travel Crisis Deepens as Europe Fears Wider Impact." April 17, 2010. http://nyti.ms/1FpSWoe (Accessed December 20, 2016.)

The PDX Project. The PDX Project. 2015. http://www.pdxcarpet.com/ (Accessed December 20, 2016.)

Uhlfelder, Eric. "The Bird-strike Threat Looms Large: With 'Sully' in Theaters, the Scary Reality is that it Could Happen Again." *New York Daily News*. September 9, 2016, 5:00 a.m. http://www.nydailynews.com/opinion/eric-uhlfelder-bird-strike-threat-looms-large-article-1.2783762 (Accessed December 20, 2016.)

Ulin, David L. "Southwest Airlines Opens Unwelcome Chapter: Writers on a Plane." *LA Times*. April 24, 2015, 10:51 a.m. http://www.latimes.com/books/jacketcopy/la-et-jc-writers-on-a-plane-20150414-story.html (Accessed December 20, 2016.)

Vanhoenacker, Mark. "Why I Love Being a Pilot." *The Guardian*. July 6, 2016. https://www.theguardian.com/travel/2016/jul/06/why-i-love-being-a-pilot-skyfaring-mark-vanhoenacker (Accessed December 20, 2016.)

Music

Bowie, David. "Starman." *The Rise and Fall of Ziggy Stardust and the Spiders from Mars*. RCA Records. 1972.

Bowie, David. "Fame." *Young Americans*. RCA Records. 1975.

Bowie, David. "★" [Blackstar]. ★ [Blackstar]. ISO, RCA Records, Columbia, and Sony. 2016.

Case, Neko. "I'm an Animal." *Middle Cyclone*. ANTI-. 2009.

Index

Note: Page numbers in italics refer to illustrations.

9/11   1, 32, 126, 130–40

Abrams, J. J.
  *Star Wars: The Force
      Awakens*   97–101, *99*, 147
advertising   105–7, 109, 115–18,
    116, 120–2, *122*, 123
Airbus   59–60, 79, 90, 100, 112,
    123, 144
Air Force One   91
airplane mode   167, *167*
airplanes   8, *25*, 32, *48*, 50–3,
        55–61, 70–3, 89–91, *90*, *110*,
        114, *123*, 139–41, 144. *See
        also* flight; plane sightings;
        individual manufacturers
  seating map   *125*
airports   2, 5, *155*
  adventure   43, 46, 157
  Americanness   166–7
  architecture and design   6, 15,
      68, 69, 159–61
  art   36–8, 157, 159
  behaviors and emotions   2–8,
      11–17, *14*, 21–30, 32–5,
      38–6, 158, 159, 165
  birds   84–7
  class-consciousness   17–20,
      26–29, 38, 154–8, *155*, 159

concourses   5, 6, 30–1, 36–8,
    47, 79, *81*
consumerism   40–3,
    154–8, *155*
contemporary culture   2–3, 5,
    7, 30, 32, 46, 165–6
curbside   12–15, *14*
environmental impact   68–9,
    130
food   2, 25, 79, 88–9, 161, 165
future   of, 2, 9, 29, 69, 159, 166
gates   25–6
imagination   159
improvements   29, 35, 68,
    89, 108
inefficiencies   39–40, 165
infrastructure   140, 164, 166
landscape   2, 68–9
media   30–3
modernity   2, 3, 7, 20, 42,
    45, 88
observation   1, 2, 29–30, 33–6,
    41–2
place lag   162–3
runways   5, 6, 43–6
scenery   84–5
security   16–17, 21–5, *24*, 33
senses   79–83, 88, 94–5
social media   161–2

submission   80–2
as symbols   2–3, 5, 32, 33
technology   16–17, 21–5, 68
time   33–5
transition   158–9
trips to and from   4–6, *14*
violence   30–3
waiting   33–5, 149, 158
as wilderness   10, 84–7
workers   13, 16–17, 25, 30, 32,
     35–6, 38, 40, 45–6, 160
"Airports: The True Cities
     of the 21st Century"
     (Ballard)   68
air rage   146–7
air travel. *See* flight
Alter, Alexandra   61
Amtrak   62
Armstrong, Neil   106
Arnold, Craig   86
   "Bird-Understander"   86–7
art   36–8, 157, 159
Asiana Airlines   100
Audi   115–17, *116*
Avatar (Cameron)   125–6, *127*,
     128, 129

baggage   154–8, *155*
Bagram, Afghanistan   90–1
Baldwin, James   95–6
   Giovanni's Room   95–6
Ballard, J. G.   68, 109
   "Airports: The True Cities of the
     21st Century"   68
   Super-Cannes   109
Barthes, Roland   54, 104–5
   Mythologies   104–5

Barton, Byron   35, 36
   Planes   35
Benjamin, Walter   136–7
   "The Work of Art in the
     Age of Mechanical
     Reproduction"   136–7
Beyond Good and Evil
     (Nietzsche)   138
birds   75–8, 84–7, 122–7, *124*, 130
"Bird-Understander"
     (Arnold)   86–7
Björk   26–7, 151, 152
"Blackstar" (Bowie)   116, 117
Black Wave (Tea)   113
Blake, William   88
Boarding Pass Shiraz   *21*
Boeing   8, 47, 79, 89–91, *90*, 96,
     100, 139–40
Bowie, David   28, 116–18, *116,*
     147–8
   "Blackstar"   116, 117
   "Starman"   116, *116*, 117
Boyega, John   98
Brody, Richard   97
Broom of the System, The
     (Wallace)   44–6
Brussels, Belgium   31
Butler, Judith   142

Cameron, James   125–6, *127*, 128,
     129
   Avatar   125–6, *127*, 128, 129
Captain America: Civil War (Russo
     and Russo)   31
Case, Neko   28
celebrity culture   91–3,
     149–51, 154

cinema vérité 132–3. *See also*
      United 93 (Greengrass)
CNN
   "Preventing another
      'Miracle on the Hudson'
      emergency" 76–7
Cohen, Jeffrey Jerome 69
   Earth 69
Columbia Performance Fishing
      Gear 42
Concorde 117
consumer culture 40–3, 105–6,
      154–8, *155*
Coppola, Sofia 93–101, *94*
   Somewhere 93–101, *94*
cosmopolitanism 32
criticism 10, 104–5, 131–2
Cruise, Tom 116
"Cyborg Manifesto, A"
      (Haraway) 140

Davis, California 112
Davis, Lydia 55–6
   "The Woman Next to Me on the
      Airplane" 55
Debord, Guy 135
DeLillo, Don 4, 22, 129
   White Noise 4, 129
   Zero K 22
Delta Airlines 40–2, *48*, 103, 114,
      131
Denver International Airport 85–
      6, 153–4
Derrida, Jacques 63
destinations 148–54
Detroit Metropolitan Wayne
      County Airport 84

Dicum, Gregory 52–3
   *Window Seat: Reading the
      Landscape from the
      Air* 52–3
discrimination 19–20, 26–9
Dooren, Thom van 75–6, 78,
      86–7
   Flight Ways 78, 86–7
Dorf, Stephen 94
Dwelling (Sawa) 109–11, *110*,
      112, 114–15

Earth (Cohen, Elkins-Tanton) 69
Eastwood, Clint
   Sully 75
ecological thinking 9–11, 130
Ecological Thought, The
      (Morton) 127–8
Elkins-Tanton, Linda T.
   Earth 69
Ellis, David R.
   Snakes on a Plane 106
End of Airports, The
      (Schaberg) 7
environmentalism. *See* ecological
      thinking
Everyone Poops (Gomi) 73
ExOfficio 42–3
extinction 86–7

Fanning, Elle 94
Farrell, Colin 91–3, 149–51, 154
fishing shirts 40–3
Fitzgerald, F. Scott 8
   "Three Hours between
      Planes" 8
Flickr 51

flight   130
  apparel   40–3
  arrivals/departures   6, 11–15, *14*, 94, 148–54, 158
  awareness   4, 7–8, 47–50, 53–5, 101–8, 133–8, 146–9, 151
  bird strikes   75–8, 86, 122–7, *124*, 130
  boarding passes   16–21, *18*
  celebrities   91–3, 149–51, 154
  classism   63–4, 91–3, 102–8
  connections   78–82, 91
  convenience   59–61
  ecosystems   11, 125–30
  emergencies   31, 32, 66–8, 75–8, 90–1, 100, 122–4, *123*, 131–9
  entertainment   93–101, *94*, *99*, 115–18, 125–7, *127*, 131–9, *135*
  fear   6, 12, 18, 50
  food   11, 16, 60, 61, 74
  frustration   2, 6, 151
  golden age   32, 166
  holding   47–9, *48*
  in-flight magazines   62, 63–7, 69, 102–3, 105–8
  involuntary   145–6
  life and culture   10–15, *14*, 50, 61–70
  merchandising   6, 7, 17–21, *18*, *21*
  modernity   8, 11, 50, 90, 101, 141, 146, 149, 161
  naturalized   8–11, 70, 79, 96, 97, 145, 151, 153, 165, 166
  observation   50–5, 108–15
  passenger interaction   50–1, 55–60, 114, 120, 124, 131, 134, 139, 141–3, 148, 152
  privacy   46, 70–3, 92, 93, 103, 124, 140, 141
  risks   22–3
  rituals/routines   1–2, 4, 5, 12–15, *14*, 16, 47, 50–4, 70, 72, 73, 74, 83, 151
  safety   17–18, *18*, 101, *118*, 118–20, *119*, 143
  sleep   1–4
  sublimity   50–3, 113, 152, 161
  takeoffs and landings   49–50, 75–8, 143–8
  terrorism   20, 30–2, 72–3, 143
  time   101–8, 130
  Westernization   152–3
  wildness   160
"Flight" (Lopez)   10
flight attendants   60, 70, 74, 75, 131, 142, 143, 147
Flight Ways (van Dooren)   78, 86–7
Ford, Harrison   98–9
frogs   143–8

Garden Rant   85
Gate Lice   39–40
gender   141–3
Gingrich, Newt   58
Giovanni's Room (Baldwin)   95–6
globalism   95–6, 164
Gomi, Taro   73
  Everyone Poops   73
Google   51, 102, 124, *124*, 125, 129

Greengrass, Paul 131–9, *135*
    United 93 131–9, *135*
Guardian 26, 28, 140, 162

Haller, Jordan 64
Haraway, Donna 140
    "A Cyborg Manifesto" 140
Heller, Nathan 157
Hemingway, Ernest 95, 96
    The Sun Also Rises 95, 96
Hemispheres 103
Heraclitus 27
Hillman, Brenda 8, 29
    "Symmetry Breaking" 8, 29
H Is for Hawk (Macdonald) 145
home 160–7
"Hostages" (Kinney) 146

Iceland 129–30
In Bruges (McDonagh) 92
Instagram 49
Istanbul, Turkey 31

Jackson, Samuel L. 102–3, 106
jetBlue *119*, 120
jet bridges 5, 47, *48*, 79
John F. Kennedy International
    Airport 128–9
Jurgenson, Nathan 161

Keats, John 157
    "Ode on a Grecian
        Urn" 157
Kinney, Alison 146
    "Hostages" 146
Kirn, Walter 152
    Up in the Air 152

lavatories 70–3, 80, 92–3, 141–2
LAX. *See* Los Angeles International
    Airport
Leed, Jessica 57–8
Legos 31–2, 160, 163–4
Linnaeus, Carl 113
Lopez, Barry 10
    "Flight" 10
Los Angeles, California 26, 28
Los Angeles International Airport
    (LAX) 26–9, *90*, 94
Los Angeles Times 62
Louis Armstrong International
    Airport 36, 37, 67–8
Louis C. K. 23, 58
    Louie 58
loyalty programs 154–8, *155*
Loyola University New
    Orleans 7–8
Lufthansa 120–2, *122*, 123,
    124, 130

McDonagh, Martin
    In Bruges 92
Macdonald, Helen 145
    H Is for Hawk 145
Mad Men 152
Mandel, Emily St. John 66–7, 69
    Station Eleven 66–7, 69
Mann, Michael
    Miami Vice 92
Man Who Fell to Earth, The
    (Roeg) 148
Marvel Super Heroes 31–2
Matrix, The (Wachowksi and
    Wachowski) 17, 40
Miami Vice (Mann) 92

Michigan   112, 141, 144
MileagePlus Explorer Chase
        VISA   *155*, 155–8
Mirror   31
Mississippi River   69
modernism/postmodernism   50,
        82, 95, 96–7, 152
modernity. *See* airports; flight
Moisant, John   67–8
    Moisant Stock Yards   67–8
Morton, Timothy   127–8
    The Ecological Thought   127–8
MSY/KMSY. *See* Louis Armstrong
        International Airport
Mythologies (Barthes)   104–5

National Airlines   90–1
Nationwide Investments,
        Retirement, and
        Insurance   17–21, *18*
New Orleans, Louisiana   36, 37,
        67, 112
New York City   123, 128, 131–9
New York Daily News   77
New Yorker   97, 120
New York Times   61–6, 107, 130
Nietzsche, Friedrich   131–3, 138
    Beyond Good and Evil   138
    "On Truth and Lying in a Non-
        moral Sense"   132

"Ode on a Grecian Urn"
        (Keats)   157
O'Hare International Airport   140
"On Truth and Lying in a
        Non-moral Sense"
        (Nietzsche)   132

Pale King, The (Wallace)   46
Patagonia   42
people-watching   29–30
Planes (Barton)   35, 36
plane sighting   108–15, *114*
play. *See* Legos; Playmobil
Playmobil   *82*, 83
poetry   86–8
Portland, Oregon   37
Portland International
        Airport   161–2

Rhapsody   63–7, 102–8, 117
Roeg, Nicolas
    *The Man Who Fell to
        Earth*   148
Russell, Karen   65
Russo, Anthony and Joe
    *Captain America: Civil
        War*   31
Ryder, Daisy   98

safety briefing cards   *18*, *118*,
        118–20, *119*
San Francisco International
        Airport   100
Saturday Night Live   23
Sawa, Hiraki   109–15, *110*
    Dwelling   109–15, *110*
Schaberg, Christopher
    The End of Airports   7
    *The Textual Life of
        Airports*   7
Scott, Tony
    Top Gun   116
Shelley, Percy   61
Sky   103

Skyfaring (Vanhoenacker)   106,
        164
Sky West Airlines   89
Smith, Charlotte   88
Snake River   22–3
Snakes on a Plane (Ellis)   106
social media   26, 49, 51, 87–8,
        151, 161
Somewhere (Coppola)   93–101, *94*
"Song of Myself" (Whitman)   40
Southwest Airlines   62, 131
space travel   115–18
"Starman" (Bowie)   116, *116*, 117
Star Wars: The Force Awakens
        (Abrams)   97–101, *99*, 147
Station Eleven (Mandel)   66–7, 69
Stevens, Wallace   112
    "Thirteen Ways of Looking at a
        Blackbird"   112
Sullenberger, Chesley (Sully)   75,
        123, 148
Sully (Eastwood)   75
Sun Also Rises, The
        (Hemingway)   95, 96
Super-Cannes (Ballard)   109
*Supposedly Fun Thing I'll Never Do
        Again, A* (Wallace)   165
"Symmetry Breaking"
        (Hillman)   8, 29

Tea, Michelle   113
    Black Wave   113
technology   7, 16, 47–9, 51, 53,
        59–61, 79–80, 82, 89–91, 93,
        100, 113, 140, *167*
television   33, 34, 80
temporality   33–5

Textual Life of Airports, The
        (Schaberg)   7
Thiebaud, Wayne   47
"Thirteen Ways of Looking at a
        Blackbird" (Stevens)   112
Thoreau, Henry David   10
"Three Hours between Planes"
        (Fitzgerald)   8
Top Gun (Scott)   116
toys. *See* Legos; Playmobil
Transportation Safety
        Administration
        (TSA)   23–4, *24*
Travis Air Force Base   112
Trump, Donald   2, 3, 8, 9, 19, 33,
        57–9, 91, 108, 117, 139–41,
        164, 165
TSA. *See* Transportation Safety
        Administration (TSA)
turtles   128–9, 130
Twitter   49, 87–8, 161

United 93 (Greengrass)   131–9,
        135
United Airlines   17–19, *18*, 102,
        104, 107, 131–9
United States   3, 56
Up in the Air (Kirn)   152
US Airways   76, 123, 148

Vanhoenacker,
        Mark   106, 162–4
    Skyfaring   106, 164
volcanoes   129–30

Wachowski, Lana and Lilly
    The Matrix   17, 40

Wallace, David Foster   44–6, 165
    The Broom of the System   44–6
    The Pale King   46
    *A Supposedly Fun Thing I'll
        Never Do Again*   165
Wall Street Journal   139
water   143–8
White Noise (DeLillo)   4, 129
Whitman, Walt   40
    "Song of Myself"   40
Williams, Terry Tempest   10
*Window Seat: Reading the
        Landscape from the Air*
        (Dicum)   52–3

Winogrand, Garry   12–14, *14*
"Woman Next to Me on the
        Airplane, The"
        (Davis)   55
"Work of Art in the Age of
        Mechanical Reproduction,
        The" (Benjamin)   136–7
World Trade
        Center. *See* 9/11
Worthington, Sam   127

YouTube   26, 151

Zero K (DeLillo)   22